Cake Mix Classics

Sensational Treats Baked The Easy Way

Geraldine Duncann

PORTLAND, OREGON

To Jessica: my granddaughter, my able apprentice, the mother of my two great-grandsons and my close, close friend.

Cover Design: Bryan Coates
Designers: Sara E. Blum, Kevin A. Welsch
Editors: Jennifer Weaver-Neist, Lindsay S. Brown

Library of Congress Cataloging-in-Publication Data

Duncann, Geraldine.
  Cake mix classics : sensational treats baked the easy way / by Geraldine Duncann. - - 1st American ed.
      p.   cm.
  Includes index.
  ISBN 1-933112-28-X (hardcover : alk. paper)
  1. Cake. I. Title.
  TX771.D864 2007
  641.8'653--dc22

                          2006028232

Distributed by Publisher Group West

First American Edition
ISBN 10: 1-933112-28-X
ISBN 13: 978-1-933112-28-2

Printed in China

9 8 7 6 5 4 3 2 1

Collectors Press books are available at special discounts for bulk purchases, premiums, and promotions. Special editions, including personalized inserts or covers, and corporate logos, can be printed in quantity for special purposes. For further information contact: Special Sales, Collectors Press, Inc., P.O. Box 230986, Portland, OR 97281. Toll free: 1-800-423-1848.

For a free catalog write to:
Collectors Press, Inc., P.O. Box 230986, Portland, OR 97281
Toll free: 1-800-423-1848 or visit collectorspress.com.

Table of Contents

Introduction

A Bit of History

There is nothing new about cake. It is referenced as far back as the ancient Phoenicians and Egyptians; the Bible mentions it in both the Old and New Testaments; and Julius Caesar even had some thoughts on the subject. Second century BC historian Agatharchides, archivist of the Ptolemys, speaks of cake, as does Greek gourmet Athenaeus, Roman gastronome Apicius, Herodotus, and Pliny the Elder (23 AD–79 AD). Centuries later, cake was certainly no stranger to Henry VIII or his daughter Elizabeth, and early American colonists would not even set foot in the New World without having their favorite cake recipes with them.

All these cakes bore little or no resemblance to what you most likely consider a cake today. These early offerings were heavy and bread-like in comparison, usually containing dried fruits, nuts, and honey as a sweetener. If they were leavened at all it would have been with yeast, as chemical leavenings like baking soda and baking powder did not come into use until much later. Some early cakes were not even baked but were made from ground nuts and/or bread crumbs that were combined with honey and spices and pressed into molds. It was the Renaissance and the Baroque era that first saw lighter cakes, which were leavened with beaten egg whites instead of yeast.

In the early nineteenth century, the introduction of chemical leavenings and affordable refined sugar revolutionized baking. The housewife no longer had to wait for yeast to rise, or go through the trouble of beating egg whites. The first chemical leavenings—introduced in the 1830s—were soda, saleratus, cream of tartar, and pearlash, which were usually used in combination with each other. Soda was the most successful, but being a base, it had to be activated with an acid such as tartar, lemon juice, vinegar, or soured dairy products. It also tended to cake when stored and had to be pounded back into a powder before it could be used. In the 1860s an acid, like cream of tartar, and a non-caking agent, like cornstarch, were added to the soda, and baking powder was born. The post-Civil War housewife was now able to whip up a light, delicate cake with ease even if she did have to chop the wood with which to bake it.

Revolution always has its detractors, however. There were clergymen and newspaper editors who ranted that the time-saving use of baking powder would lead to the breakdown of the family unit and civilization itself. They preached that women using baking powder instead of yeast or egg whites would have far too much time on their hands, thus falling prey to the temptations of the devil. They predicted that these "lazy and slothful" women would take to drink, gambling, and worse yet, seek employment outside the home, thus neglecting their husbands and children. Fortunately few husbands were concerned, finding the benefits of the lighter cakes easily outweighed the potential demise of the social structure around them.

Like chemical leavenings and refined sugar, the Industrial Revolution brought other time saving devices to the kitchen. The first dry mix was developed in England with the introduction of a powdered custard mix in the 1840s. Packaged gelatins like Jell-O, Royal, and Knox were introduced in the 1880s and 90s. The first baking mixes however did not make an appearance until the 1930s with the introduction of Bisquick.

The first packaged cake mixes did not hit the market until the late 1940s. Mixes had been developed for the military during World War II, but use in the home only became popular after the war. And they were not well received at first. Manufacturers had assumed that after four years of liberation from her domestic duties, Rosie the Riveter would be loathed to exchange her work clothes for an apron and to get back into the kitchen full time. Surely she would eagerly embrace the time saving opportunity cake mixes offered. They were wrong. At first Rosie was very glad to get back to her home full time, and those early mixes were mediocre at best. The manufacturers had made them a little too instant; all you had to add was water. Cake mixes did not become widespread until the powdered egg and dehydrated shortening were removed from the mix, requiring the addition of oil and fresh eggs. Not only did this produce a far superior cake, but the public felt it was authentic—like the ones grandma use to make from scratch.

Since their introduction, cake mixes have gone through many changes. Numerous types have been introduced, kept on the market for a time, then eliminated. One example was a "Honey Spice mix," introduced in 1953 and receded in 1973. (Don't ask me how they got real honey in the box!) Another example of a flash in the cake pan was the "Answer Cake," introduced in 1964. This was an all-in-one package containing the cake mix, the baking dish, and the frosting. It was off the market by 1968, and its reappearances since have been short lived.

Always on the quest for a richer and moister cake, mixes have gone through numerous changes with various additions and subtractions. Some have been packaged with pudding, some with fruits, and others with their own fillings. These miracle specialties arrive with a lot of promise, stay on the grocers' shelves for a few years, then vanish to make room for some new twist on the quicker and better theme. Interestingly the popularity of the basic three mixes—white, spice, and chocolate—never seems to diminish.

Author's Thoughts

Cake mixes in American kitchens have become the norm after sixty years of use. The bugs have certainly been worked out, and creative marketing and culinary experimentation has taken them out of the realm of simply being a convenience. Home cooks can now use cake mixes to make a myriad of delectable "home-baked" treats, and it is my hope that the recipes in this book will help to bring ingenuity and creativity into your kitchen.

In preparation for writing this book, I brought home a white, spice, and devil's food cake mix from each of the three major producers—Betty Crocker, Pillsbury, and Duncan

Hines—and made the cakes following the directions precisely. I found that there was absolutely no difference among any of the major brands, so start with whichever brand is more readily available or on sale. I also experimented with some lesser-known brands—brands that still included the desiccated shortening and powdered eggs—and found the cakes less than rewarding.

With few exceptions the recipes in this book use white, spice, or devil's food cake mixes. I found these were the mixes that were available in almost every market. You may certainly use canned or packaged icings or frostings, but frosting is very easy to make, as you'll see from the recipes supplied in this book. You will also find recipes in the book for related enhancements, like streusel topping and baker's syrup. If you bake a lot, both are great to keep on hand in the refrigerator or freezer. They help to give your baked goods that real, homemade finishing touch.

Here are dozens of recipes for delectable homemade baked goods, appropriated from a variety of cultures. Using a mix as a starting point, you will be able to create everything from old-fashioned favorites such as Red Velvet Cake and Banana Nut Cake, to incredible creations like a Viennese Sachertorte or a Sicilian Wedding Cake. You'll find homey standards like Fresh Apple Upside Down Cake, Streusel Coffee Cake, and Molasses Swirls. There is even Seedy Cake from England, Porter Cake from Ireland, and Apfelkuchen from Switzerland. All are delicious and easy to make, but I am sorry to say, none are low calorie. So enjoy indulging your sweet tooth to the fullest.

Sweet Tips for Success

Pan Preparation for Cakes

There are three major ways to prepare your pans for baking:

● Oil the pan and dust it with flour. Turn the pan upside down and tap to remove excess flour.

● Spray with nonstick cooking spray.

● Cut parchment paper to fit the bottom of the pan and spray the sides with nonstick cooking spray. Parchment paper is excellent but won't work for pans like Bundts pans of course. You can purchase it at specialty baking supply stores, craft stores that have a cake decorating department, wholesale restaurant supply houses, and online. Prices will vary greatly.

Pan Preparation for Cupcakes

Lining the muffin pans with paper baking cups makes cupcakes easier to get out of the baking tins; however, unless you spray the papers with nonstick cooking spray, they are very hard to peel off the cupcakes.

Always Do the Toothpick Test

No matter what the power company and the oven manufacturer say, not all ovens are the same. An oven at 350°F for 30 minutes means one thing in one oven and quite another thing in another. Use the baking time listed as a guideline, not an absolute. Always insert a toothpick into the center to know for sure. If the toothpick comes out clean, the cake is done.

Mixing Batter

All these recipes call for an electric mixer. If you prefer, you may beat your cake by hand. No matter what the method, always stop partway through the mixing and scrape down the sides before proceeding.

Cooling Cakes

Wire cake racks are a good investment. It is a good practice to place your cakes on wire racks to cool as soon as they come out of the oven. If you have no wire racks, place the hot cake pan on two chopsticks or wooden spoons to allow air to circulate around them, thus promoting the cooling process.

Splitting/Cutting Layers

Several recipes in this book call for splitting or cutting the cake in half to create thinner layers. Sometimes the cake mounds up too much during baking and you need to remove the top to make the cake or layer more level. For round cakes, the most successful way to do this is to gently place the palm of one hand on top of the cake. Then hold the blade of a very sharp, non-seriated, knife horizontally against the cake at the level where you wish to make the cut. Gently turn the cake about a quarter turn, lift your hand, place it back on top of the cake, give another quarter turn, and continue in this manner until the cake is cut all the way through. This makes it easer to make the two halves even than if you just put the knife on one side and start cutting.

Frosting a Cake

● Always dust off all crumbs before beginning to frost a cake.

● To keep the cake plate clean, cut 3 or 4 strips of waxed paper about 4 inches wide. Lay the strips around the edge of the cake plate in such a way that part of each piece will be under the cake, and part will extend beyond the cake to protect the plate. Frost the cake as usual. When finished, gently pull the pieces of wax paper from under the cake and you are left with a perfectly clean plate.

● When frosting a cake that is multi-layered, always reserve the best looking, most even layer to use for the top layer of the cake.

● You may use canned frosting if you wish, however I have provided recipes for the frostings used in this book.

How to Slice a Cake

Many times people destroy a lovely cake by placing the knife on top of it and just pressing down when they cut it. This compacts the crumb of the cake. To properly slice a cake, use a very sharp, slim-bladed knife (never seriated) and use a gentle sawing motion. If the cake is at all gooey or has frosting, it is a good idea to have a moist cloth handy to wipe the blade clean after each slice.

Cakes and Loaves

Is it possible to have a birthday without a birthday cake? Not for most families. A cake usually means something special is happening. Easter may feature a cake shaped like a bonnet, and a red, white, and blue cake with sparklers is its own celebration for the Fourth of July. Then there is devil's food cake and pumpkin ice cream for Halloween, and Christmas wouldn't be Christmas without a rich, dark, brandy-soaked fruit cake.

And don't forget about filled cakes, tube cakes, and other variations. These scrumptious creations are most definitely not your everyday cake, depending on delectable fillings, shapes, glazes, or unique ingredients to leave an impression.

Whether hollow, filled, frosted, or glazed, a cake makes any day memorable and delicious!

Lazy-Dazy Cake

Traditional Lazy-Dazy cakes were the invention of busy farm wives who did not have time to mess around with frosting their cakes. Instead they mixed together brown sugar, coconut flakes, chopped nuts, and butter, spread it on top of the cake, and popped it in the oven to melt into a yummy, candy-like topping.

Serves 8 to 10

Cake:

1 (18 1/4-ounce) package white cake mix

3 large eggs

1/3 cup vegetable oil

1 cup water

Topping:

1 cup sugar

2 tablespoons molasses

1 cup coconut flaked, sweetened or unsweetened

1/2 cup chopped walnuts

1 teaspoon ground cinnamon

1/2 teaspoon ground nutmeg

1/2 teaspoon powdered ginger

1/4 cup (1/2 stick) butter

1/4 cup milk

1. Preheat the oven to 350°F. Prepare a 9- or 10-inch springform pan.

2. To make the cake, combine the cake mix, eggs, oil, and water in a large bowl. With an electric mixer set on medium speed, mix the ingredients together for about 2 minutes, until all the ingredients are thoroughly combined.

3. Pour the batter into the prepared pan and bake for 30 to 35 minutes, until a toothpick inserted into the center comes out clean.

4. Prepare the frosting while the cake is baking. Combine the sugar, molasses, coconut flakes, walnuts, cinnamon, nutmeg, ginger, butter, and milk in a large saucepan and cook over medium heat, stirring constantly, until the butter is melted and all the ingredients are well mixed.

5. As soon as the cake comes out of the oven, pour the warm topping over the surface of the cake and spread evenly.

6. Set the oven to broil on medium-high and return the cake to the oven. Leave for 3 to 4 minutes or until the topping is lightly browned.

7. Remove the cake from the oven and allow it to cool. Remove the sides of the springform pan and slide the cake onto a serving plate. Slice and serve.

Handy Hint: If you don't have a broiler option on your oven, turn the oven to 450°F or 500°F.

Fresh Apple Upside-Down Cake

Upside-down cakes are another busy farm-wife creation. She just opened a jar of the fruit she canned last autumn, added the contents to the baking dish before the batter, and her cake had a lovely topping when it was turned out of the dish. This version, using fresh apples instead of canned, is the essence of harvest season.

Serves 8 to 10

Topping:

2/3 cup sugar

1/4 cup (1/2 stick) butter

1 tablespoon ground cinnamon

1 teaspoon ground nutmeg

1/2 teaspoon ground allspice

1/2 teaspoon ground ginger

1 to 2 large crisp apples, such as Fuji, Granny Smith, or Pippin, peeled, cored, and thinly sliced

Cake:

1 (18 1/4-ounce) package white cake mix

3 large eggs

1/3 cup vegetable oil

1 cup water

1. Preheat the oven to 350°F. Prepare a 9- or 10-inch springform pan. (Note: This cake is best if you spray the pan thoroughly with nonstick cooking spray, place a circle of parchment paper in the bottom, and then spray the parchment with the cooking spray.)

2. To make the topping, combine the sugar, butter, cinnamon, nutmeg, allspice, and ginger in a small saucepan. Stir over medium heat until the butter is melted and the ingredients are well mixed. Pour into the bottom of the prepared pan.

3. Arrange the sliced apples evenly in the bottom of the pan; set aside.

4. To make the cake, combine the cake mix, eggs, oil, and water in a large bowl and blend with an electric mixer at medium speed for 2 minutes. Gently pour the batter over the apples in the pan.

5. Bake the cake for 45 minutes or until a toothpick inserted into the center comes out clean.

6. Remove the cake from the oven and cool for a bit. Before completely cool, remove the outer ring of the springform pan. Set a serving plate on top of the cake and carefully invert. Remove the bottom of the pan, then slowly and carefully peel the parchment from the cake. If any of the apple topping sticks to the paper, scrape it off with a knife and replace it on the top of the cake. (Note: If the cake is completely cold, it will become difficult to remove the paper without having the topping stick to it.)

7. Cool completely, slice, and serve.

California Gold Loaf

You will think you have struck gold when you bite into this sunny loaf! It is a delicious treat that brings a bit of California's sun to a winter table with its crop of golden raisins, apricots, orange marmalade, and almonds.

Serves 10 to 12

1 (18 1/4-ounce) package white or yellow cake mix

2 large eggs

1/3 cup vegetable oil

1 cup water

1 cup golden raisins

1 cup finely chopped dried apricots

1 cup chopped almonds

1 cup orange marmalade

1. Preheat the oven to 350°F. Prepare two 5 x 9-inch loaf pans.

2. Combine the cake mix, eggs, oil, and water in a large bowl and blend with an electric mixer at medium speed for about 2 minutes.

3. Fold in the raisins, apricots, and almonds with a wooden spoon.

4. Divide the batter evenly between the prepared pans.

5. Spoon the marmalade onto the batter and swirl it in with a table knife or chopstick. The object is not to thoroughly incorporate it into the batter. You want to be able to bite into little pockets of marmalade.

6. Place the pans in the center of the oven and bake for 30 to 35 minutes, until a toothpick inserted into the centers comes out clean.

7. Remove the loaf pans from the oven and cool completely before turning the loaves out of the pans. Slice and serve or wrap and store. This moist cake will keep for at least a week.

Handy Hint: Most loaves and cakes will keep for several days, but if you live where there is high humidity, they should be refrigerated.

Lemon Cake

This is a delicious and unusual cake. It has a delightful lemony flavor and the texture is a little denser than a standard cake. The secret ingredient is unsweetened lemonade-flavored Kool-Aid!

Serves 8 to 10

2 (.23-ounce) packages unsweetened lemonade drink mix, such as Kool-Aid

1 cup water

1 (18 1/4-ounce) package white, yellow, or lemon cake mix

3 large eggs

1/3 cup vegetable oil

Zest of 1 medium lemon

Yellow food coloring (optional)

Confectioners' sugar, to serve (optional)

1. Preheat the oven to 350°F and prepare a Bundt pan.

2. Dissolve the drink mix in the water.

3. Combine the lemonade mixture, cake mix, eggs, oil, and lemon zest in a large bowl and blend with an electric mixer at medium speed for about 2 minutes. If you wish, add a drop or two of yellow food coloring and blend until an even color is achieved.

4. Pour the batter into the prepared pan and place in the center of the oven. Bake for 30 to 35 minutes, until a toothpick inserted into the center comes out clean.

5. Remove the cake from the oven and allow to cool.

6. When completely cooled, turn the cake out onto a serving plate. Lightly dust the top with confectioners' sugar, if using, for a nice finishing touch. Slice and serve.

Piña Colada Cake

Delectably moist and bespeaking all the tropical delights of its namesake, this rich cake is a real crowd pleaser. Make it for you next summer get-together. A coconut variation follows.

Serves 8 to 10

1 (18 1/4-ounce) package white cake mix

3 large eggs

1/3 cup vegetable oil

3/4 cup canned coconut milk

1 cup coconut flakes, sweetened or unsweetened, plus more for serving

1 (8-ounce) can crushed pineapple, drained and with juice reserved

1/2 cup chopped Macadamia nuts, plus more for serving

1/2 cup dark rum

2 tablespoons butter

Buttercream frosting (page 48)

1. Preheat the oven to 350°F. Prepare two 8- or 9-inch round cake pans.

2. Combine the cake mix, eggs, oil, and coconut milk in a large bowl and blend with an electric mixer at medium speed for 2 minutes.

3. Fold in the coconut flakes, pineapple, and Macadamia nuts with a wooden spoon.

4. Divide the batter evenly between the prepared pans and bake in the center of the oven for about 30 minutes or until a toothpick inserted into the center of each cake comes out clean.

5. While the cakes are baking, put the reserved pineapple juice, rum, and butter in a small saucepan over high heat and bring to a boil. Reduce the heat to a simmer and cook for about 5 more minutes.

6. When the cakes come out of the oven, pour the rum-pineapple syrup over them and cool completely before removing them from the pans.

7. When completely cooled, frost with buttercream frosting. Sprinkle some coconut flakes and/or crushed macadamia nuts on the top. Slice and serve.

Coconut Cake: *Follow the directions for making Piña Colada Cake, but use 1 cup of canned coconut milk and eliminate the pineapple, nuts, and rum-pineapple syrup. Frost the cake with Buttercream frosting and coat the sides and top generously with coconut flakes.*

Handy Hint: Can size is irrelevant when buying coconut milk, which is a different liquid than that found inside a coconut. Most brands are imports, and their can sizes vary greatly.

Strawberry Torte

This very unique filled cake is a spectacular creation for a special occasion. Its fresh strawberry filling and delicate whipped cream topping make it perfect for a sweet sixteenth birthday party, a wedding shower, or a celebration announcing the arrival of spring and the start of strawberry season.

Serves 10 to 12

Cake:

1 (18 1/4-ounce) package white cake mix

4 large eggs

1/3 cup vegetable oil

1 teaspoon almond extract

1/2 teaspoon ground nutmeg

1 cup water

Filling:

1 (3-ounce) package strawberry gelatin

1 cup boiling water

1 pint heavy cream

1 pint strawberries, hulled and thinly sliced with a few reserved whole for garnish

1. Preheat the oven to 350°F. Prepare three 8- or 9-inch round cake pans.

2. To make the cake, combine the cake mix, eggs, oil, almond extract, nutmeg, and water in a large bowl and blend with an electric mixer at medium speed for about 2 minutes.

3. Divide the batter evenly between the prepared pans and bake in the center of the oven for about 25 minutes or until a toothpick inserted into the centers comes out clean.

4. Remove the cakes from the oven and cool completely.

5. While the cakes are cooling, prepare the filling. Put the gelatin in a medium bowl and add the boiling water. Whisk until completely dissolved. Refrigerate until thickened but not completely set, like extra thick cream. You will need to keep an eye on it and stir it now and then to prevent a skin from forming on the bottom of the bowl.

6. When the gelatin is the right consistency, whip half of the cream in a separate medium bowl and fold it into the gelatin. Fold in the sliced strawberries with a wooden spoon, then return it to the refrigerator.

7. Remove the cakes from their pans and dust off any loose crumbs. Carefully slice each cake into two thin layers.

8. Set a layer on a cake plate and spread with one-fifth of the strawberry filling. Top with another layer of cake and spread with another one-fifth of the filling. Continue in this manner but do not spread the strawberry filling on the top layer. (Note: It does not matter if some of the filling oozes out between the layers of cake.)

9. Whip the remaining cream and use it to frost the top. Garnish with the reserved whole berries and chill before serving.

Plantation Cake

This cake was typical of the plantation era, when most of these establishments maintained their own stills for making medicinal and culinary spirits. When home-brewed whiskey was combined with pecans, molasses, and a simple spice cake, the result was this delectably moist treat. This is excellent served with strong coffee "sweetened" with a splash of bourbon.

Serves 8 to 10

1 (18 1/4-ounce) package spice cake mix

3 large eggs

1/3 cup vegetable oil

1/3 cup dark molasses

1 cup bourbon

1 cup chopped pecans

Coffee frosting (page 49)

Pecan halves, to serve

1. Preheat the oven to 350°F. Prepare two 8- or 9-inch round cake pans.

2. Combine the cake mix, eggs, oil, molasses, and bourbon in a large bowl and mix with an electric mixer at medium speed for about 2 minutes. Fold in the pecans with a wooden spoon.

3. Divide the batter evenly between the prepared pans. Place in the center of the oven and bake for 30 to 35 minutes, until a toothpick inserted in the centers comes out clean.

4. Remove the cakes from the oven and cool before removing from the pans.

5. Place one layer on a decorative plate and spread a layer of coffee frosting on top. Put the other cake layer on top of the frosting and frost the top and sides. Decorate the top cake with pecan halves and serve.

Handy Hint: Use the same implement for measuring molasses that you used when you measured the oil, and the molasses will come away easily, leaving no sticky mess behind.

Doboschtorte

Here is a sinful specialty from Vienna. It is from an era when coffee houses were vying with each other for customers by creating incredibly delectable pastries. The layers of this fine cake are separated by chocolate pudding, and all is topped by a sugary glaze.

Serves 16

Cake:

1 (18 1/4-ounce) package white cake mix

4 large eggs

1/2 cup (1 stick) butter, melted and cooled

1 tablespoon vanilla extract

1 cup water

Filling:

1 (3.4-ounce) package instant chocolate pudding

1 cup milk

1/2 cup heavy cream

Glaze:

1 cup sugar

1/3 cup water

1. Preheat the oven to 350°F. Prepare three 8- or 9-inch round cake pans.

2. To make the cake, combine the cake mix, eggs, butter, vanilla extract, and water in a large bowl and blend with an electric mixer at medium speed for about 2 minutes.

3. Divide the batter evenly between the prepared pans and bake in the center of the oven for 25 to 30 minutes, until a toothpick inserted into the centers comes out clean. Remove from the oven and cool completely before turning out of the pans. The result will be three, rather thin cakes.

4. To make the filling, combine the pudding mix and milk in a separate large bowl and whisk until thoroughly blended. Continue to whisk until thickened, about 2 minutes. Set aside.

5. Whip the cream in a medium bowl until it holds stiff peaks. Gently fold the cream into the pudding and chill.

6. Carefully cut each of the cooled cakes into two layers and dust off any crumbs. Choose the best-looking of the layers and set aside. Place one of the layers, cut side down, on a cake plate and spread with one-fifth of the filling. Top with another layer and spread with the filling. Continue with the remaining three layers, ending with a filling layer on top.

7. Place the reserved layer on a wire rack set over a baking sheet and set aside.

8. To make the glaze, combine the sugar and water in a small saucepan and stir over medium-high heat until the sugar is completely dissolved. Allow the mixture to come to a boil and, without stirring but swirling the pan periodically, continue to cook until the mixture becomes a caramel color.

9. Remove the pan from the heat and pour over the layer of cake on the wire rack. Allow it to run into a smooth, even topping. Immediately use a butter knife to score the topping into 16 equal wedges. You want to score through the topping but not cut into the cake.

10. Using two spatulas or bench knives, gently lift the layer and place it on top of the cake. Slice along the score marks and serve.

Bûche de Noël (Yule Log)

The roots of this classic French Christmas cake reach back to pagan days, when it was traditional to burn a Yule log on the dark winter solstice, the shortest day of the year, as an effort to entice the sun to return. The tradition gradually transformed into this tasty creation. A variation follows.

Serves 10 to 12

1 (18 1/4-ounce) package white cake mix

6 large eggs

1/3 cup water

2 tablespoons orange-flavored liqueur, plus more to taste

Sifted confectioners' sugar

1/2 pint heavy cream

2 tablespoons sugar

Chocolate fudge frosting (page 48)

About 1/2 cup finely chopped walnuts

Evergreen sprigs, to serve

Tiny pinecones, to serve

Artificial spotted mushrooms, to serve

1. Preheat the oven to 350°F. Prepare a standard jelly roll pan by spraying with nonstick cooking spray, covering the bottom of the pan with parchment paper, and spraying again with the cooking spray.

2. Combine the cake mix, eggs, and water in a large bowl and blend with an electric mixer at medium speed for about 3 minutes.

3. Pour the batter into the prepared pan and bake in the center of the oven for 12 to 15 minutes, until a toothpick inserted into the center comes out clean. It is crucial not to over bake this cake.

4. As soon as the cake comes out of the oven, sprinkle the top generously or to taste with orange-flavored liqueur.

5. Lay a clean tea towel or piece of muslin on top of the cake and invert the pan; remove the parchment paper. Using a sharp knife, trim off the edges evenly. Working quickly, sprinkle the top of the cake generously with confectioners' sugar. While the cake is still warm and flexible, start at the short side and roll it loosely into a log. You want to roll the cloth with it. Set aside to completely cool.

6. Meanwhile, pour the heavy cream into a medium bowl and beat until it holds soft peaks. Sprinkle the sugar and 2 tablespoons liqueur over it and continue beating until it holds firm peaks.

7. Roll another tea towel or two into logs and have ready. Carefully unroll the cake most of the way; do not try to lay it flat or it will crack. Prop the end of the cake that was in the center (the more tightly rolled end) up with the rolled up tea towels. This will help prevent the cake from cracking. Remove the towel that was in the center. Quickly spread the whipped cream over the entire surface of the cake and carefully roll it back up. It may crack in a few places, but the frosting will cover it.

8. With two broad spatulas or bench knives, carefully lift the roll onto a decorative serving plate. Use a table knife to remove any cream that may have oozed out of either end.

9. Carefully frost with the fudge frosting, using the frosting to mask any places where the cake may have cracked. While the frosting is still soft, use a fork to draw irregular lines to represent rough bark. Scatter the chopped nuts here and there to represent lichens and moss.

10. Use the sprigs of evergreen to decorate the cake plate and garnish the cake with the miniature pinecones and mushrooms. Keep chilled until ready to slice and serve.

Jelly Roll: Follow the directions for baking Bûche de Noël using a white or yellow cake mix. When the cake comes out of the oven, turn it out of the pan and remove the parchment paper. Spread a favorite jelly or jam on top and roll it while still warm. Allow to completely cool, then place on a decorative plate, sprinkle with confectioners' sugar, and serve sliced.

Handy Hint: You can purchase artificial mushrooms during Christmas time, when most places that sell ornaments also sell little bundles of mushrooms for decorating use.

English Seedy Cake

Seedy Cake is a favorite English teatime treat. In England the seeds used are almost always caraway seeds; few Americans are enamored with caraway, so you may use poppy or sesame seeds instead. This cake is traditionally baked in fluted tube pans. This is the perfect "little something" to have with tea.

Serves 10 to 12

1 (18 1/4-ounce) package spice cake mix

3 large eggs

1/3 cup vegetable oil

1 1/3 cups water

2 tablespoons seeds of choice, such as caraway, poppy, sesame, or anis

2 teaspoons ground cinnamon

1 teaspoon ground nutmeg

1/2 teaspoon ground ginger

1/2 teaspoon ground cardamom

Warm baker's syrup (page 46)

Confectioners' sugar, to serve (optional)

1. Preheat the oven to 350°F. Prepare two 7-inch fluted tube pans or pan(s) of choice.

2. Combine the cake mix, eggs, oil, water, seeds, cinnamon, nutmeg, ginger, and cardamom in a large bowl and blend with an electric mixer at medium speed for 2 minutes.

3. Divide the batter evenly between the prepared pans and bake in the center of the oven for 30 to 35 minutes, until a toothpick inserted into the centers comes out clean.

4. Remove the cakes from the oven and paint liberally with the baker's syrup. Cool completely before removing from the pans.

5. Place the cakes on decorative plates and top each with a dusting of confectioners' sugar, if using. Slice and serve.

Handy Hint: If you do not have 7-inch fluted tube pans, you may use one large tube pan (angle food cake pan) or Bundt pan.

Dublin Porter Cake

This scrumptious, rich, dark, and moist cake is typical of the cakes baked in pre-World War II Ireland. It was traditionally baked in a round tube pan, but you may use two loaf pans if you wish. Do not use a Bundt pan because the nuts and raisins will make it difficult to remove.

Serves 12 to 16

1 (18 1/4-ounce) package spice cake mix

3 large eggs

1/3 cup vegetable oil

1 cup Guinness or other dark beer

1 tablespoon ground cinnamon

1 teaspoon ground nutmeg

1 teaspoon ground cardamom

1/2 cup dark raisins

1/2 cup coarsely chopped walnuts

About 1/2 cup warm baker's syrup (page 46)

1. Preheat the oven to 350°F. Prepare a tube pan or two 5 x 9-inch loaf pans.

2. Combine the cake mix, eggs, oil, Guinness, cinnamon, nutmeg, and cardamom in a large bowl and mix with an electric mixer at medium speed for 2 minutes. Fold in the raisins and walnuts with a wooden spoon.

3. Pour the batter into the prepared pan and bake in the center of the oven for 45 to 50 minutes (30 to 35 if using loaf pans), until a toothpick inserted into the center comes out clean.

4. Remove the pan from the oven and immediately pour the warm baker's syrup evenly over the cake.

5. When completely cooled, run a knife around the edge of the pan and turn out onto a serving plate. This cake is best if stored in an airtight container for 2 to 3 days before slicing and serving.

Molasses Walnut Cake

Old-fashioned and versatile, this cake is another farmhouse classic. Molasses was less expensive than sugar, and most households had a jug on hand in the pantry. Sugar was reserved for canning and special occasions. The liberal use of eggs in this recipe also allowed a farm wife to show off her productive hen house.

Serves 8 to 10

1 (18 1/4-ounce) package spice cake mix

4 large eggs

1/4 cup (1/2 stick) butter, melted and cooled

1 tablespoon ground cinnamon

1 teaspoon ground ginger

1 teaspoon ground nutmeg

1/4 teaspoon ground cloves

1/2 cup molasses

2/3 cup buttermilk

1 cup chopped walnuts, plus more chopped or halved for garnish

Coffee frosting (page 49)

1. Preheat the oven to 350°F. Prepare two 8- or 9-inch round cake pans.

2. Combine the cake mix, eggs, butter, cinnamon, ginger, nutmeg, cloves, molasses, and buttermilk in a large bowl and blend with an electric mixer at medium speed for 2 minutes. Fold in the walnuts with a wooden spoon.

3. Divide the batter evenly between the prepared pans and bake in the center of the oven for about 30 to 35 minutes, until a toothpick inserted into the centers comes out clean.

4. Remove the cakes from the oven and cool completely.

5. Take the cakes out of the pans and dust off any loose crumbs. Layer and frost with coffee frosting, decorating with a sprinkling of chopped nuts or with nut halves placed around the outer edge of the cake. Slice and serve.

Streusel Coffee Cake

As easy as it is delectable, this hot and spiced treat is a delicious way to greet the day. Serve warm from the oven, accompanied by rich, strong coffee and perhaps a bit of extra heavy cream poured over the top. Four variations follow.

Serves 6 to 8

1 (18 1/4-ounce) package spice cake mix

3 large eggs

1/3 cup vegetable oil

1 cup water

About 2 cups streusel topping (page 47)

About 1/2 cup warm baker's syrup (page 46)

1. Preheat the oven to 350°F. Prepare a 9 x 13-inch baking dish.

2. Combine the cake mix, eggs, oil, and water in a large bowl and blend with an electric mixer at medium speed for about 2 minutes.

3. Pour the batter into the prepared dish and sprinkle the streusel topping evenly over the top.

4. Bake for 35 to 40 minutes, until a toothpick inserted into the center comes out clean.

5. Remove the cake from the oven and immediately pour the warm baker's syrup evenly over the top. Cool for about 5 minutes before slicing into squares and serving.

Fresh Blueberry Coffee Cake: Gently fold 1 cup fresh blueberries into the batter for Streusel Coffee Cake and complete the recipe as directed. You may replace the blueberries with a cup of any fresh soft fruit such as blackberries, raspberries, chopped peaches, apricots, or strawberries.

Pumpkin-Spice Coffee Cake: Fold 1 cup canned pumpkin, 1 tablespoon ground cinnamon, 1 teaspoon ground nutmeg, and 1 teaspoon ground ginger into the batter for Streusel Coffee Cake. Complete the recipe as directed.

Italian Cheese Coffee Cake: In Streusel Coffee Cake, gently fold 1 cup ricotta cheese and 1 teaspoon fennel seeds into the batter. Complete the recipe as directed.

Apple Sauce Coffee Cake: Stir 1 teaspoon ground cinnamon, 1/2 teaspoon ground ginger, and 1/2 teaspoon ground nutmeg into 1 1/2 cups apple sauce. Spread over the top of the batter for Streusel Coffee Cake instead of the streusel topping. Complete the recipe as directed.

Kona Coffee Cake

Crowned with streusel topping and flavored by macadamia nuts, spices, and coconut flakes, this Hawaiian inspired breakfast treat not only goes well with coffee but also has coffee in it.

Serves 6 to 8

1 cup streusel topping (page 47)

1/2 cup chopped macadamia nuts

1/2 cup coconut flakes, sweetened or unsweetened

1 (18 1/4-ounce) package spice cake mix

3 large eggs

1/4 cup (1/2 stick) butter, melted and cooled

1 cup strong-brewed Kona coffee or other dark roast coffee, cold

About 1/2 cup warm baker's syrup (page 46)

1. Preheat the oven to 350°F. Prepare a 9- or 10-inch springform pan or cast iron skillet.

2. Mix together the streusel, nuts, and coconut flakes in a medium bowl and set aside.

3. Combine the cake mix, eggs, butter, and coffee in a large bowl and blend with an electric mixer at medium speed for 2 minutes.

4. Pour the batter into the prepared pan and sprinkle the streusel-nut mixture evenly over the top.

5. Bake in the center of the oven for 35 to 40 minutes, until a toothpick inserted into the center comes out clean.

6. Remove the cake from the oven and pour the baker's syrup evenly over the top. Cool for about 5 minutes before slicing and serving.

Truly Delectable Holiday Fruit Cake

Everyone gets fruitcake for Christmas and no one ever eats it. This is a fruitcake that changes all that.
The trick is to avoid commercial fruit cake mix, to make the cake in July, and to age it with brandy.
Believe me, this is a fruitcake they will eat! Serve in small slices, as it is rich and heady.

Serves 16 to 20

1 (18 1/4-ounce) package spice cake mix

3 large eggs

1/4 cup (1/2 stick) butter, melted and cooled

1 tablespoon ground cinnamon

1 teaspoon ground nutmeg

1 teaspoon ground ginger

1/2 teaspoon ground cardamom

1/4 teaspoon ground cloves

1 cup strong-brewed dark roast coffee, cold

1 cup orange marmalade

1/2 cup coarsely chopped walnuts

1/2 cup coarsely chopped almonds

1/2 cup coarsely chopped filberts

1/2 cup coarsely chopped Brazil nuts

1/2 cup coarsely chopped pecans

1/2 cup dark raisins

1/2 cup golden raisins

1/2 cup currants

1/2 cup pitted and chopped dates

1/2 cup chopped dried figs

1/2 cup chopped dried apricots

1/2 cup chopped candied ginger

1 cup warm baker's syrup (page 46)

1 cup brandy or holiday brandy-rum mix, plus more for marinating

1. Preheat the oven to 350°F. Prepare a 9- or 10-inch tube pan (not a Bundt pan) or three 5 x 9-inch loaf pans.

2. Combine the cake mix, eggs, butter, cinnamon, nutmeg, ginger, cardamom, cloves, and coffee in a large bowl and blend with an electric mixer at medium speed for about 2 minutes. Add the marmalade, nuts, raisins, currants, dates, figs, apricots, and candied ginger and fold into the batter using a wooden spoon.

3. Pour the batter into the prepared pan, then set the pan inside a larger pan and place in the center of the oven.

4. Fill the larger pan half-full with boiling water. Bake for about 1 to 1 1/2 hours, until a toothpick inserted into the center of a cake comes out clean. Refill the larger pan with boiling water when necessary.

5. Remove the cake from the oven and set aside to cool.

6. Meanwhile, mix the baker's syrup with 1/2 cup of brandy in a small bowl and pour evenly over the cake while it is still hot. Cool completely before removing the cake from the pan.

7. Remove the cake from the pan and wrap it in clean cotton or muslin cloths. Pour about 1/2 cup of additional brandy over the cloths and place the wrapped cakes in an airtight plastic container.

8. Put the container away for at least three months. About twice a month, pour a bit more brandy over the cloths. This cake can be kept for months—even years—because of the alcohol, and it gets better and better with time.

Handy Hint: If you can only get inspired to make a fruitcake during the holidays, make it then and age it until next year.

29

Maple Swirl Cake

This old-fashioned New England cake was traditionally served at "sugaring off" parties, when the newly made maple syrup was further reduced and poured into pans to sugar. It was a community event similar to a barn raising, and the thick syrup produced was used to make a variety of delicious creations like this one.

Serves 8 to 10

1 (18 1/4-ounce) package spice cake mix

3 large eggs

1/4 (1/2 stick) butter, melted and cooled

1/2 cup water

1 1/2 cups pure maple syrup

Crushed maple sugar, to serve (optional)

Unsweetened whipped cream, to serve (optional)

1. Preheat the oven to 350°F. Prepare a Bundt pan.

2. Combine the cake mix, eggs, butter, water, and 1/2 cup of maple syrup in a large bowl and blend with an electric mixer at medium speed for about 2 minutes.

3. Pour the batter into the prepared pan and bake in the center of the oven for 30 to 35 minutes, until a toothpick inserted into the center comes out clean.

4. Remove the cake from the oven and set aside to cool.

5. While the cake is cooling, place the remaining maple syrup in a medium saucepan over high heat and bring to a boil. Immediately reduce the heat to a rapid simmer and continue to cook until reduced to about half of its volume.

6. Turn the cake out onto a serving plate and drizzle with the reduced maple syrup. Top with crushed maple sugar and/or a dollop of whipped cream, if using, and serve.

Holiday Eggnog Cake

Enhanced with a touch of holiday cheer, this unique cake is just the thing for end-of-the-year celebrations. Eggnog, brandy, and spices are among its ingredients, and a simple topping of confectioners' sugar keeps the cake from becoming too rich.

Serves 8 to 10

1 (18 1/4-ounce) package spice cake mix

1/3 cup vegetable oil

3 large eggs

1 cup eggnog

1 teaspoon ground nutmeg

1/4 cup brandy, or to taste

Sifted confectioners' sugar, to serve

1. Preheat the oven to 350°F. Prepare a Bundt pan.

2. Combine the cake mix, oil, eggs, eggnog, and nutmeg in a large bowl and blend with an electric mixer at medium speed for about 2 minutes.

3. Pour the batter into the prepared pan and bake in the center of the oven for 30 to 35 minutes, until a toothpick inserted into the center comes out clean.

4. Remove the cake from the oven and pour the brandy over it. Allow it to cool completely before turning out of the pan.

5. Invert the cake onto a serving plate and dust the top lightly with confectioners' sugar. Slice and serve.

Handy Hint: Decorate the platter with freshly washed evergreen sprigs, and you have a welcome addition to any holiday sideboard or buffet table.

Banana-Nut Cake

When bananas were first introduced from Hawaii, they were not very popular. It took the creation of banana nut cake to make them a standard household item. Frosted or plain, the recipe has been a favorite since the 1930s.

Serves 8 to 10

1 (18 1/4-ounce) package spice cake mix

3 large eggs

1/3 cup vegetable oil

1 cup water

2 ripe medium bananas, peeled and mashed

1 cup coarsely chopped walnuts

Coffee frosting (optional; page 49)

Walnut halves, to serve (optional)

1. Preheat the oven to 350°F. Prepare a 9 x 11-inch baking dish.

2. Combine the cake mix, eggs, oil, and water in a large bowl and blend with an electric mixer at medium speed for about 2 minutes. Fold in the bananas and walnuts with a wooden spoon.

3. Pour the batter into the prepared dish and bake in the center of the oven for 30 to 35 minutes, until a toothpick inserted into the center comes out clean.

4. Remove the cake from the oven and allow it to cool completely before turning it out onto a serving plate.

5. Serve as is, or frost the top and sides of the cake with coffee frosting. You can also score the frosting while it is still moist, creating squares or diamonds and placing a walnut half, if using, inside each one.

White Lightning Cake

This moist, unfrosted loaf is an old-time recipe dating from a time when you either had your own still for brewing alcohol or you knew someone who did. Since "white lightning" isn't available or legal, you may substitute apple brandy. This is in essence an applesauce cake, but it uses fresh apples as well as applesauce.

Serves 10 to 12

1 (18 1/4-ounce) package spice cake mix

3 large eggs

1/3 cup vegetable oil

2/3 cup water

1/3 cup plus 1/4 cup apple brandy

1 cup applesauce

2 large crisp apples, such as Fuji, Granny Smith, or Pippins, peeled, cored, and chopped

1/4 cup warm baker's syrup (page 46)

1. Preheat the oven to 350°F. Prepare two 5 x 9-inch loaf pans.

2. Combine the cake mix, eggs, oil, water, 1/3 cup brandy, and the applesauce in a large bowl and blend with an electric mixer at medium speed for about 2 minutes. Then fold in the chopped apples with a wooden spoon.

3. Divide the batter evenly between the prepared pans and bake in the center of the oven for 30 to 35 minutes, until a toothpick inserted in the centers comes out clean.

4. Remove the cakes from the oven and set aside to cool.

5. Mix the baker's syrup and remaining brandy together in a small bowl, then pour the mixture over the cakes while they are still hot.

6. Cool completely before removing from the pans. Slice and serve.

Handy Hint: Slices of unfrosted cake are an excellent item for the lunch box.

Zucchini Cake

What do you do with all the zucchini neighbors won't accept any more? Why, make this moist and delicious cake, of course! A summertime classic and a gardener's delight, this recipe uses up two small zucchinis in a few simple steps. Two variations using carrot and pumpkin follow.

Serves 10 to 12

1 (18 1/4-ounce) package spice cake mix

3 large eggs

1/3 cup vegetable oil

1/3 cup dark molasses

1 teaspoon ground cinnamon (optional)

1 teaspoon ground nutmeg (optional)

1/2 teaspoon ground ginger (optional)

1 cup water

1 cup grated zucchini (about 2 small)

1 cup chopped walnuts (optional)

Warm baker's syrup (page 46)

1. Preheat the oven to 350°F. Prepare two 5 x 9-inch loaf pans.

2. Combine the cake mix, eggs, oil, molasses, spices (if using), and water in a large bowl and blend with an electric mixer at medium speed for about 2 minutes. Fold in the zucchini and walnuts with a wooden spoon.

3. Divide the batter evenly between the prepared pans and bake in the center of the oven for 30 to 35 minutes, until a toothpick inserted in the centers comes out clean.

4. Remove the cakes from the oven and paint the tops generously with baker's syrup.

5. Cool the cakes before removing them from the pans, then slice and serve.

Carrot Cake: *Substitute 1 cup grated carrot for the zucchini in the Zucchini Cake, then proceed with the recipe as directed.*

Pumpkin Cake: *Substitute 1 cup canned pumpkin for the zucchini in Zucchini Cake, then proceed with the recipe as directed. (Note: You may use baked and mashed acorn squash or Hubbard squash in place of the canned pumpkin.)*

Hazelnusstorte

The Viennese Empire isn't through with your waist yet! Flavored with hazelnuts and coffee liqueur, this scrumptious creation is guaranteed to brighten up any coffee klatch or tea party.

Serves 10 to 12

1 (18 1/4-ounce) package spice cake mix

4 large eggs

1/4 cup (1/2 stick) butter, melted and cooled

1 cup water

1 cup ground hazelnuts

Coffee liqueur, to taste

1/2 pint heavy cream

Sugar, to taste

1/2 cup finely chopped hazelnuts

1. Preheat the oven to 350°F. Prepare a 10-inch springform pan.

2. Combine cake mix, eggs, butter, and water in a large bowl and blend with an electric mixer at medium speed for about 2 minutes. Fold in the cup of hazelnuts with a wooden spoon.

3. Pour the batter into the prepared pan and bake in the center of the oven for 30 to 35 minutes, until a toothpick inserted into the center comes out clean.

4. Remove the cake from the oven and cool completely before turning out of the pan.

5. Carefully cut the cake into two equal layers. Place the layers, cut side up, and sprinkle with coffee liqueur to taste.

6. In a medium bowl, whip the cream until it holds stiff peaks. Sweeten to taste with sugar and coffee liqueur.

7. Place the bottom layer, cut side down, on a cake plate. Spread an even layer of whipped cream on the top, then place the top layer, cut side down, on top of that. Frost the top and sides with the remaining whipped cream and sprinkle chopped hazelnuts on the top and sides. Chill until ready to serve.

Swiss Apfelkuchen

Here is a very tasty twist on the applesauce cake theme. The base is a cake filled with apples and hazelnuts and moistened with apple brandy, and the filling is a tasty blend of custard and applesauce.

Serves 8 to 10

2 large crisp apples, such as Fuji, Granny Smith, or Pippins, peeled, cored, and chopped

1 tablespoon ground cinnamon

1 teaspoon ground nutmeg

1/2 teaspoon ground ginger

1/4 cup sugar

1 (18 1/4-ounce) package spice cake mix

3 large eggs

1/3 cup vegetable oil

1 cup water

1 cup chopped hazelnuts

1/4 cup apple brandy, plus more for baking

1 (3- to 4-ounce) package instant vanilla pudding

1 cup milk

1 cup applesauce

Sifted confectioners' sugar, to serve

1. Preheat the oven to 250°F. Prepare three 9- or 10-inch round cake pans.

2. Put the apples, cinnamon, nutmeg, ginger, and sugar in a medium bowl, toss, and set aside.

3. Combine the cake mix, eggs, oil, and water in a large bowl, then blend with an electric mixer at medium speed for about 2 minutes. Fold in the apple-spice mixture and the hazelnuts with a wooden spoon.

4. Divide the batter evenly between the prepared pans and bake in the center of the oven for 20 to 25 minutes, until a toothpick inserted into the centers comes out clean. The result will be three, rather thin cakes.

5. Remove the cakes from the oven and sprinkle generously with apple brandy, to taste. Cool completely before removing from the pans.

6. Meanwhile, combine the pudding mix and milk in a medium bowl and wisk until well blended. Continue blending until the mixture has thickened. Fold in the applesauce and the 1/4 cup of apple brandy and set aside.

7. When the cakes are cool, remove them from their pans and dust off all the crumbs. Choose the best-looking cake and set aside.

8. Place one cake on a serving plate and spread half of the applesauce-pudding mixture on the top. Place the second cake on the filling, then spread the remaining filling on top of it. Add the reserved layer and sprinkle the top with confectioners' sugar. Don't worry if some of the filling oozes out between the layers. Slice and serve.

Mississippi Red Velvet Cake

This classic cake, with its strong southern associations, is a delight to serve. Hiding under its snow white frosting is a rich, moist cake, the color of deep red velvet draperies.

Serves 12 to 15

1 (18 1/4-ounce) package Dutch chocolate cake mix

3 large eggs

1/3 cup vegetable oil

1 cup buttermilk

Red food coloring (enough to turn the batter a deep red)

Cream cheese frosting (page 47)

Chopped pecans and pecan halves, to serve

1. Preheat the oven to 350°F. Prepare two 8- or 9-inch round cake pans.

2. Combine the cake mix, eggs, oil, buttermilk, and food coloring in a large bowl and blend with an electric mixer at medium speed for about 2 minutes.

3. Divide the batter evenly between the prepared pans and bake in the center of the oven for 30 to 35 minutes, until a toothpick inserted in the centers comes out clean.

4. Take the cakes out of the oven and set aside to cool completely before removing from the pans.

5. Meanwhile, make the frosting.

6. To assemble, remove the cooled cakes from their pans and dust off any loose crumbs. Cut the layers in half horizontally and set aside the nicest one for the top layer.

7. Place one layer, cut side down, on a cake plate and spread an even layer of frosting. Continue in this manner, always placing the cut side down. Place the reserved layer on top and frost the top and sides evenly and carefully. Coat the sides generously with the chopped pecans and place the pecan halves about 1-inch apart around the outer edge of the top of the cake. Slice and serve.

Sachertorte

Sachertorte is one of the unbelievably rich and flavorful, completely decadent treats served in the coffee houses of Vienna. You can hear a Strauss waltz and see fashionable ladies swirling around the dance floor with every bite. Its chocolate glaze, dense cake, and layers of apricot jam make it so rich that it should be served in very thin slices.

Serves 12 to 16

Cake:

1 (18 1/4-ounce) package devil's food cake mix

4 large eggs

1/2 cup (1 stick) butter, melted and cooled

1 tablespoon vanilla extract

1 tablespoon ground cinnamon

1 cup water

Chocolate glaze:

1 large egg

3 ounces (3 squares) baker's chocolate, finely chopped

1 cup heavy cream

1 cup sugar

1 teaspoon light corn syrup

1 tablespoon vanilla extract

Coffee-flavored liqueur, to taste

About 2 cups apricot jam

Whipped cream, to serve

1. Preheat the oven to 350°F. Prepare two 8- or 9-inch round cake pans.

2. To make the cake, combine the cake mix, eggs, butter, vanilla extract, cinnamon, and water in a large bowl and blend with an electric mixer at medium speed for about 2 minutes.

3. Divide the batter evenly between the prepared pans and bake in the center of the oven for 25 to 30 minutes, until a toothpick inserted into the centers comes out clean.

4. Remove the cakes from the oven and cool completely.

5. Meanwhile, make the glaze. Beat the egg in a small bowl and set aside. Combine the chocolate, cream, sugar, and corn syrup in a medium saucepan and stir over medium heat until melted. Adjust the heat to maintain a rapid simmer and continue to cook, stirring constantly, until the soft ball stage is reached (approximately 240°F on a candy thermometer).

6. Remove the saucepan from the heat and slowly pour about 1/2 cup of chocolate mixture into the beaten egg, whisking all the while. Pour the egg mixture back into the chocolate mixture and continue whisking.

7. Reduce the heat to low and whisk for another 3 to 4 minutes, until the mixture has thickened.

8. Remove the saucepan from the heat and whisk in the vanilla extract. Cool to room temperature, whisking occasionally to prevent a skin from forming on the top.

9. To assemble, remove the cakes from their pans and dust off any crumbs. Place the layers on a flat surface and cut each into two equal layers. Dust off any additional crumbs.

10. Sprinkle each of the 4 layers generously or to taste with the coffee flavored liqueur.

11. Place one layer, cut side down, on an 8- or 9-inch cardboard cake disk. Place the disk on a wire rack placed over a baking sheet.

12. Warm the jam in the microwave for about 30 seconds, then spread one-third of it evenly over the surface of the first cake layer. Place another layer, cut side up, on top and spread with another one-third of the jam on top. Repeat with the third layer and top with the remaining layer, cut side down.

13. Pour the chocolate glaze over the top of the cake and spread evenly. Allow it to run over the edge to coat the sides evenly. When it has stopped dripping, use two large spatulas or two bench knives and gently lift the cake onto a cake plate. As if this wasn't rich enough, Sachertorte is traditionally served with a generous dollop of whipped cream flavored with coffee liqueur.

Handy Hint: Cardboard cake disks are available at specialty baking and candy making shops and at some craft supply stores.

Double Chocolate Walnut Rum Cake

Here is a chocolate cake that truly deserves the name! Bursting with chocolate and walnuts
and enhanced with rum, it's the "he-man's" chocolate cake.

Serves 10 to 12

4 ounces (2 squares) baker's chocolate, chopped small

1/4 cup (1/2 stick) of butter

2 (18 1/4-ounce) packages devil's food cake mix

8 large eggs

2 cups water

2 tablespoons ground cinnamon

2 tablespoons vanilla extract

2 cups coarsely chopped walnuts

1/2 cup warm baker's syrup (page 46)

1/3 cup rum

Chocolate fudge frosting (page 48)

About 1 1/2 cups finely chopped walnuts

Walnut halves, to serve

1. Preheat the oven to 350°F. Prepare three 8- or 9-inch round cake pans.

2. Melt the chocolate and butter in a medium saucepan over low heat and set aside to cool.

3. Combine the cake mix, eggs, water, cinnamon, vanilla extract, and butter-chocolate mixture in a large bowl and blend with an electric mixer at medium speed for about 3 minutes.

4. Fold in the walnuts with a wooden spoon and divide the batter evenly between the prepared pans. Bake in the center of the oven for 30 to 35 minutes, until a toothpick inserted into the centers comes out clean.

5. As soon as the cakes come out of the oven, combine the baker's syrup and rum in a small bowl. Pour the mixture evenly over the three cakes and allow them to cool completely before removing from the pans.

6. Remove the cooled cakes from their pans and set aside the most attractive layer for the top.

7. Cut the remaining 2 layers across their tops if they rose into high mounds while baking. Place one of the layers, cut side down, on a cake plate and spread the fudge frosting evenly on the top. Stack the second layer on top of the frosting and follow with another layer of frosting. Add the top layer, rounded side up, then frost the top and sides.

8. Coat the sides of the cake with the chopped walnuts, then place the walnut halves about an inch apart around the outer edge of the cake. Slice and serve.

Black Forest Chocolate Cherry Cake

This sinful creation is deep in chocolate flavor and enhanced by a surprise filling of black cherries. And if that isn't enough, it is iced with a fluffy cloud of whipped cream frosting. Try it accompanied by a cup of equally rich coffee or espresso.

Serves 10 to 12

1 (18 1/4-ounce) package devil's food cake mix

3 large eggs

1/4 cup (1/2 stick) butter, melted and cooled

1 cup water

2 ounces (2 squares) baker's chocolate, finely chopped and melted

1 (15- or 16-ounce) can pitted black cherries, drained

Kirsch (cherry flavored brandy), to taste

1 (1.9- or 2-ounce) package instant chocolate pudding

1 1/2 cups milk

1 (21 ounce) can cherry pie filling

Whipped cream frosting (page 49)

Handy Hint: An easy way to pipe pudding or frosting with everyday kitchen supplies is to seal the frosting in a sealable plastic bag and snip off one corner of the bag with scissors. Simply squeeze out through the hole.

1. Preheat the oven to 350°F. Prepare three 8- or 9-inch round cake pans.

2. Combine the cake mix, eggs, butter, water, and melted chocolate in a large bowl and blend with an electric mixer at medium speed for about 2 minutes. Fold in the cherries, reserving some for decoration.

3. Divide the batter evenly between the prepared pans and bake in the center of the oven for 25 to 30 minutes, until a toothpick inserted in the centers comes out clean.

4. Remove the cakes from the oven and sprinkle generously with Kirsch. Cool completely before turning out of the pans.

5. Meanwhile, combine the pudding mix and milk in a medium bowl and whisk until well blended. Continue blending until the mixture has thickened. Refrigerate until needed.

6. Place one cake layer on a cake plate. Pipe a ring of the pudding about half an inch thick around the cake's outer rim. Spread half of the can of pie filling inside the ring of pudding. Top with a second cake layer and repeat the process. Place the third layer on top and refrigerate while you make the frosting.

7. Before frosting the cake, use a table knife to scrape off any of the filling that may have oozed out from between the layers. Frost the top and sides generously with the frosting and arrange the reserved cherries in the center or around the edge of the cake. Serve chilled.

Chocolate Decadence Cake

This is a truly sinful concoction that should be reserved for those days when you are feeling particularly self-indulgent. You will not believe anything this good can be so easy. Four variations follow, though you may use any combination of cake mix and instant pudding to create your own variations.

Serves 8 to 10

1 (3- to 4-ounce) package instant chocolate pudding

1 1/2 cups milk

1 (18 1/4-ounce) package devil's food cake mix

3 large eggs

1/3 cup vegetable oil

1 cup water

1/2 cup warm baker's syrup (page 46)

1/4 cup rum

Whipped cream, to serve

1. Preheat the oven to 350°F. Prepare a Bundt pan.

2. Combine the pudding mix and milk in a medium bowl and wisk until well blended. Continue blending until the mixture has thickened. Set aside.

3. Combine the cake mix, eggs, oil, and water in a large bowl and blend with an electric mixer at medium speed for about 2 minutes.

4. Pour the batter into the prepared pan and spoon the prepared pudding on top. Do not stir it in.

5. Bake in the center of the oven for 35 to 40 minutes, until a toothpick inserted into the center comes out clean.

6. Remove the cake from the oven and set aside to cool.

7. In a small bowl, mix together the baker's syrup and rum and pour the mixture over the cake while it is still warm.

8. Allow the cake to cool for about 5 minutes before turning out onto a serving plate. Serve warm or cold with a dollop of whipped cream alongside each slice.

Lemon Pudding Cake: Replace the devil's food cake mix in Chocolate Decadence Cake with lemon cake mix and the zest of 2 medium lemons. Use instant lemon pudding mixed with the zest of 1 medium instant of the chocolate pudding. Add the juice of 1 medium lemon to the baker's syrup instead of rum and complete the recipe as directed.

Vanilla Cream Cake: Replace the devil's food cake mix in Chocolate Decadence Cake with either yellow or white cake mix. Use instant vanilla pudding instead of the chocolate pudding. Leave out the rum and complete the recipe as directed.

Coconut Cream Cake: Replace the devil's food cake mix in Chocolate Decadence Cake with yellow cake mix combined with 1 cup coconut flakes, sweetened or unsweetened. Use instant vanilla pudding made with 1 cup canned coconut milk instead of the chocolate pudding. Complete the recipe as directed.

Rum-Plum Cake: Replace the instant chocolate pudding in Chocolate Decadence Cake with instant vanilla pudding mixed with 1 teaspoon rum and 1/2 cup plum preserves with Complete the recipe as directed.

Handy Hint: For a special occasion, pile the whipped cream into the center of the cake and slice the cake at the table.

English Trifle

This delicious creation got its name because it is such a "trifling" thing to make. When guests dropped in unexpectedly, you could whip up this dessert by moistening stale cake with a bit of sherry or brandy, spreading it with jam, and topping it with a bit of pudding and whipped cream.

Serves 10 to 12

1 (16-ounce) package pound cake mix or Pseudo Pound Cake (page 50)

2 large eggs

1 cup water

1 teaspoon almond extract

About 1/4 cup cream sherry or brandy, or to taste

2 cups milk

1 (3- to 4- ounce) package instant vanilla pudding

1 teaspoon vanilla extract

About 2 cups raspberries or sliced strawberries (fresh or frozen)

1 to 2 tablespoons sugar (optional), plus more to taste

About 1/2 cup raspberry or strawberry jam or preserves

1/2 pint heavy cream

Handy Hint: It is best but not absolutely necessary to make the pound cake a day or two before you assemble.

1. Preheat the oven to 335°F. Prepare a 5 x 9-inch loaf pan.

2. Follow the Pseudo Pound Cake recipe on page 50 or combine the pound cake mix, eggs, water, and almond extract in a large bowl and blend with an electric mixer at medium speed for about 2 minutes.

3. Pour the batter into the prepared pan and bake in the center of the oven for 30 to 35 minutes, until a toothpick inserted in the center comes out clean.

4. Remove the cake from the oven and cool completely.

5. Cut the cake into 1/4-inch-thick slices, lay them flat on a plate, and sprinkle each slice with the sherry. Set aside to soak.

6. Put the milk in a medium bowl and sprinkle the pudding mix over it. Whisk until completely incorporated. Add the vanilla extract and continue to whisk for about 2 minutes, until the pudding has thickened. Set aside.

7. Hull the strawberries, if using, and slice them if they are large. Put the berries in a medium bowl and sprinkle with the 1 to 2 tablespoons of sugar, if using. Reserve a few of the best-looking berries to use as a garnish. Set aside.

8. Spread each slice of pound cake with a thin layer of jam and arrange in the bottom of a large, glass serving bowl.

9. Spread a layer of the pudding over the cake and sprinkle a few berries on top of the pudding. Top this with another layer of the cake, more pudding, and more berries. Continue in this manner until all the ingredients are used, ending with the pudding and berries on top.

10. Whip the cream in a medium bowl and sweeten to taste with sugar. Drop dollops of the whipped cream on the trifle and garnish with a few whole berries. Serve chilled.

Sicilian Wedding Cake

Traditional at Sicilian weddings, this cake is a loaf and not the mile-high constructions we tend to associate with American weddings. Do not be fooled by its simplistic presentation, however. Hidden inside its humble exterior is a medley of delectable flavors.

Serves 8 to 10

1 (16-ounce) package pound cake mix or Pseudo Pound Cake (page 50)

2 large eggs

1 cup water

1 tablespoon vanilla extract

Orange liqueur, to taste

1/2 pint heavy cream

Sugar, to taste

1 cup ground hazelnuts

Chocolate fudge frosting (page 48)

Handy Hint: If you are making the Pseudo Pound Cake to make this recipe, you will only need to use one of the loaves. Freeze the left over loaf for future use.

1. Preheat the oven to 345°F. Prepare a 5 x 9-inch loaf pan.

2. Follow the Pseudo Pound Cake recipe on page 50 or combine the cake mix, eggs, water, and vanilla extract in a large bowl and blend with an electric mixer at medium speed for about 2 minutes. Pour the batter into the prepared pan and bake in the center of the oven for 30 to 35 minutes, until a toothpick inserted in the center comes out clean.

3. Remove the cake from the oven and completely cool before turning out of the pan.

4. Cut the cake into 4 equal horizontal layers. Sprinkle the layers generously with the orange-flavored liqueur and set aside to soak.

5. Whip the cream in a medium bowl until very stiff. Add sugar and orange liqueur, to taste, then fold in 3/4 cup of hazelnuts. Set aside.

6. Place one layer of the cake, cut side down, on an attractive serving plate. Spread with one-third of the flavored whipped cream on the top. Gently add another cake layer, and spread with another one-third of the cream. Top this with a third cake layer and spread on the remaining whipped cream. Gently lay the last layer on top and refrigerate until the cream is firm.

7. While the cake is chilling, make the fudge frosting.

8. Remove the cake from the refrigerator and use a table knife to scrape away any of the whipped cream that has oozed out from between the layers. Frost the cake generously with the frosting, then scatter the remaining hazelnuts on top while the frosting is still soft.

9. Chill before slicing and serving.

Filled Sponge

In England a basic cake-like pound cake is called a "sponge," and the filled sponge is very popular. It is a simple cake of choice split into two layers to sandwich a yummy filling. Traditionally they are not frosted, but occasionally the tops are dusted with confectioners' sugar or cocoa powder.

Serves 8 to 10

1 (16-ounce) package pound cake mix or cake mix of choice

Filling of choice, such as whipped cream, lemon custard, chocolate pudding, jam, or preserves

Confectioners' sugar or cocoa powder, to serve (optional)

1. Bake the pound cake in a prepared 8- or 9-inch springform pan according to the manufacturer's directions. Set aside to cool.

2. When the cake is completely cooled, remove from the pan and cut it horizontally to form a top layer and a bottom layer.

3. Spread your filling of choice carefully on the top side of the bottom layer. Top the filling with the top layer, cut side down. Sprinkle confectioners' sugar over the top, if using, and serve.

Handy Hint: Make a Christmas Filled Sponge by folding crushed candy canes or whole cranberry sauce into the whipped cream filling.

Baker's Syrup

Baker's syrup is a handy thing to have around, turning a rather mundane cake into a real treat. It will keep indefinitely in the refrigerator and can be heated in the microwave when you are ready to use it.

Makes about 4 cups, enough to frost a 3 layer cake generously

1 cup sugar

1 cup water

1/4 cup (1/2 stick) butter

1 tablespoon vanilla extract

1. Bring all the ingredients to a boil in a medium saucepan over medium heat. Reduce the heat to a simmer and continue to cook for about 5 minutes. Use warm to enhance baked goods.

Streusel Topping

This is a very useful item to have around, and this recipe makes more than you will need for one cake. Put what is left in an airtight container and store in the freezer indefinitely. You will find that you are more likely to whip up a tasty coffee cake or batch of muffins if you already have the streusel topping made.

Makes about 8 cups

1 (18 1/4-ounce) package spice cake mix

2 cups sugar

1 cup quick-cooking oats

2 tablespoons ground cinnamon

1 teaspoon ground nutmeg

1 teaspoon ground ginger

1 teaspoon ground allspice

2 cups (4 sticks) butter cut into small pieces

1. Combine the cake mix, sugar, oats, cinnamon, nutmeg, ginger, and allspice in a large bowl and mix well.

2. With your hands, thoroughly incorporate the butter into the dry ingredients. Use as directed or store in the freezer for a future use.

Handy Hint: When you have trimmings from cakes, cupcakes, or muffins, crumble them and store in an airtight container in the freezer. Use the crumbles to make streusel topping. Streusel, which comes from the German "to strew," is not a precise recipe. You can use the stale crumbs to replace all or part of the cake mix in the recipe given here.

Cream Cheese Frosting

Makes 3 to 4 cups, enough for one 9-inch, 4-layer cake

1 (8-ounce) package cream cheese, softened

1/4 cup shortening (white in color)

1 1/2 pounds confectioners' sugar, sifted

1 teaspoon almond extract

Milk

1. Combine the cream cheese and shortening in a large bowl and blend with an electric mixer at medium speed until light and fluffy.

2. Add the confectioners' sugar and extract and begin blending. While blending, add the milk, 1 teaspoon at a time, until a creamy consistency is achieved; the amount of milk needed will vary greatly.

Buttercream Frosting

Makes about 4 cups, enough to frost a 3 layer cake generously

2 pounds sifted powdered sugar

1/2 cup (1 stick) butter, softened

1 tablespoon vanilla (or flavoring of choice)

Milk

1. Put the powdered sugar into a large mixing bowl.

2. Add the softened butter and vanilla or other flavoring

3. Begin mixing with an electric mixer at the slowest speed, adding the milk 1 tablespoon at a time until you have achieved a smooth spreadable consistency. It is necessary to begin with the mixer set at the lowest setting or you will throw powdered sugar all over the kitchen. As you add the liquid you may gradually increase the speed.

Chocolate Fudge Frosting

Makes 3 to 4 cups, enough for one 9-inch, 3-layer cake

2 pounds confectioners' sugar, sifted

1/2 cup (1 stick) butter

4 ounces (4 squares) semisweet chocolate

1 tablespoon vanilla extract

About 6 tablespoons half-and-half

1. Put the confectioners' sugar in a medium bowl and set aside.

2. In a small saucepan melt the butter and chocolate together over medium-low heat.

3. Pour the chocolate mixture into the confectioners' sugar, then mix in the vanilla extract.

4. Begin mixing with an electric mixer at medium speed, adding the half-and-half, 1 tablespoon at a time, until you have a smooth, spreadable consistency.

Handy Hint: Leftover frosting may be stored in a sealable plastic bag in the refrigerator for as long as it tastes good. If you have several different colors of frosting leftover, store them all together in the same zip lock bag or refrigerator dish. You can later mix them together and use them for making chocolate frosting by adding melted baker's chocolate or powdered chocolate.

Coffee Frosting

Makes about 4 cups, enough to frost a 3 layer cake generously

2 pounds sifted powdered sugar

1/2 cup (1 stick) butter, softened

1 teaspoon ground coffee

1 teaspoon vanilla

Strongly-brewed dark roast coffee, cold

1. Put powdered sugar into a large bowl.

2. Add the butter, ground coffee, and vanilla.

3. Begin mixing with an electric mixer set at the lowest speed. Add the cold coffee 1 tablespoon at a time, until you have achieved a smooth, spreadable consistency. It is necessary to begin with the mixer set at the lowest setting or you will throw powdered sugar all over the kitchen. As you add the liquid you may gradually increase the speed.

Handy Hint: Use dark roast beans that have been ground on the espresso or Turkish setting of the grinder.

Whipped Cream Frosting

Makes 3 to 4 cups, enough for a 9-inch, 3-layer cake

1/4 cup water

1 teaspoon unflavored gelatin

1/2 pint heavy cream

1 tablespoon sugar

2 tablespoons Kirsch (cherry flavored brandy)

Red food coloring (optional)

1. Put the water in a small saucepan and sprinkle the gelatin over the surface. Leave until completely softened (can take anywhere from 5 to 20 minutes). Cook over low heat and stir gently until dissolved. Set aside.

2. In a medium bowl, whip the cream until it holds soft peaks. Begin adding the softened gelatin, sugar, and Kirsch and continue whipping until it holds firm peaks.

3. If you wish, use just a drop of red food coloring to tint the frosting a very pale pink.

Pseudo Pound Cake

If you cannot find pound cake mix, you may make a reasonable facsimile as follows. A true pound cake is made with one pound of flour, one pound of sugar, one pound of butter, and one pound (8 to 10) of eggs. When making pound cake for use in a trifle or other such dessert, it is best to make it a day in advance. The texture is better for slicing.

Makes two 9 x 5-inch loafs

8 large eggs

1 tablespoon finely grated lemon peel

1 tablespoon lemon juice

1/2 teaspoon ground nutmeg

1 (18 1/4-ounce) package white or yellow cake mix

1/2 cup (1 stick) butter, melted and cooled

1. Preheat the oven to 325°F. Prepare two 9 x 5-inch loaf pans.

2. Put the eggs in a large bowl and beat with an electric mixer at medium speed for about 3 minutes, until frothy and somewhat thickened. Add the lemon peel, lemon juice, and nutmeg and beat until well incorporated. Add the cake mix and blend for about 2 minutes. Add the butter and blend for 30 more seconds.

3. Divide the batter evenly between the prepared pans and bake in the center of the oven for 35 to 40 minutes, until a toothpick inserted into the centers comes out clean.

4. Remove the cakes from the oven, turn out of the pans, and set aside to cool. Serve immediately or save for a later use.

Handy Hint: If you are using the Pseudo Pound Cake to make the English Trifle, you will only need to use one of the loaves. Freeze the leftover for future use. For a quick and easy dessert try serving the cake with a scoop of ice cream, a bit of chocolate syrup, a scoop of sweetened berries, or even a drizzle of a brandy or favorite liqueur, like Kahlua.

Special Occasions

The following are a few suggestions for sprucing up your cakes on special occasions.

Confetti Cake

Children's Birthday Parties, New Year's Eve/Day, Anniversaries, Showers

Use white cake mix to make this cake, and leave it white or tint it a pastel shade with a few drops of food coloring. Gently fold about 1/4 cup of multi-colored cake decorations into the batter. The best type is the little flat disks that are about 1/8-inch in diameter. Frost the cake with a pastel-tinted frosting or leave it white and sprinkle a few of the confetti decorations on the top as well.

You can achieve another fun confetti effect by putting some coconut flakes in a sealable plastic bag and adding just a drop of food coloring. Close the bag and knead it until the coconut is evenly colored. Make three or four different colors and use them to decorate the cake.

Carousel Cake

Children's Birthday Parties, May Day, Baby Showers

Everyone loves a carousel, so why not have one for your next special occasion? Using springform pans, bake one 9- or 10-inch layer cake and one 6-inch layer cake. Frost the top and sides of the large layer with white or pastel-tinted frosting. Center the small layer on the top of the larger one and frost. Stand animal crackers around the sides of the smaller layer. Cut out a circle of bright-colored construction paper about 14 inches in diameter and scallop the edges. Cut a 2- to 3-inch-wide pie-shaped wedge out of the circle at the outer edge. Use invisible tape and tape the cut edges together on the underside. Bend the scallops down to form the top of the carousel. Insert a brightly colored or striped drinking straw into the cake where each of the animal crackers are. Place one straw in the center of the cake. Slip a slim bamboo skewer, point end up, into each straw. Carefully set the paper carousel top on the points of the skewers and mark where each skewer touches it. Punch a small hole at each mark and gently set the top on the skewers so that one sticks through each hole. You want the skewers to stick up through the top about an inch. Cut small triangular pennons from construction paper and glue or tape one to each skewer.

Marble Cake
Birthday Parties, Fourth of July, Halloween

To make a marble cake, you need two or three different colored batters. Divide the cake batter into two or three bowls and tint each with a different food coloring. When filling the prepared cake pans, put some of each color batter in each pan. Use a table knife or chopstick to swirl the batters and make a marbled pattern. Do not over mix, as the colors will blend together.

Marble cakes are usually made of chocolate and white batters, but you can get creative with your own variations. For the Fourth of July, divide white cake mix batter into three bowls and color one red, one blue, and leave one white. Use chocolate batter and an orange-colored batter for Halloween, or tint two to three small bowls of light-colored batter in pastel colors to celebrate a birthday or the coming of spring. You can even marble-ize the frosting by piping thin lines of contrasting frosting on top of the frosted cake and gently dragging a table knife or toothpick through the lines to create a marbled effect.

In the case of a marbled chocolate and white cake, you will need to use two mixes—one chocolate and one white. It will make a larger than normal cake or two smaller ones. You can also use three 8- or 9-inch round pans, three 5 x 9-inch loaf pans, a Bundt, or Angel-food tube pan.

Checkerboard Cake

Birthdays, Anniversaries, Nascar or Grand Prix Parties
There are sets of special pans available at specialty shops for making a checkerboard cake. Follow the directions that come with the pans. When using mixes, you will need to use two boxes. Tint each batter a different color just like you would with a marble cake. The usual combinations are chocolate cake and vanilla cake, though there are plenty of other color combinations for other holidays and occasions. Let your imagination be your guide.

Easter Bonnet Cake

Easter, Showers, Birthdays
In a springform pan, bake one 9- or 10-inch layer cake; this will be the brim. In a small

ovenproof bowl (5 or 6 inches in diameter at the top), bake the crown. Line a cake plate with a paper lace doily and set the brim on it. Frost with pastel-colored frosting, then set the crown on top but all the way to one side of the brim. Frost the crown as well. Place a ribbon around the crown and tie into a perky bow at the back or side of the bonnet. Using artificial or real flowers, decorate your spring bonnet. Be sure to use flowers that are at least not toxic, if not edible. Good choices are very small roses (Cecil Bruner), forget-me-nots, pansies, small daisies, geraniums, and orange blossoms.

Tiered Cakes

Weddings, Anniversaries, Birthdays

There are special sets of pans that make beautiful three-tiered cakes. Most of the sets will require two boxes of mix. Since decorating can be quite involved and time consuming, it is perfectly fine to freeze the tiers until you are ready to frost and assemble them. Just allow adequate time for thawing before you proceed.

King Cake

Twelfth Night, Mardi Gras, Birthdays

Traditionally king cake or Mardi Gras cake is a sweet yeast bread, however you can have a festive facsimile using a favorite cake mix. Bake any flavor cake in a Bundt pan. Frost the cake with a thin coat of buttercream frosting (page 48), and decorate it with colored sprinkles or sugar in the traditional Mardi Gras colors: bright yellow, green, and purple. The colored sugar should be applied quite heavily in stripes about 2 inches wide all around the cake. A nice finishing touch is to scatter some sprinkles and/or sugar around the cake plate when the cake is finished. It is traditional to bake a coin into the cake. The person who finds it in his or her slice is king (or queen) for the day. Do not do this for children, as there is too much risk of choking. Also, for sanitation, wrap the coin in aluminum foil.

Watermelon Cake

Summer Picnics, Potlucks, Barbecues

You will need to make this cake in an ovenproof bowl. Use a white mix, leaving one-quarter of it white and the rest pink. Add a handful of currants to the pink batter. Prepare the bowl with the oil and flour method (page 9), then use a rubber spatula to spread the white batter on the bottom and sides of the bowl. Quickly pour in the pink batter. Bake at 350°F for about 30 to 35 minutes or until a slim bamboo skewer inserted into the center comes out clean. Allow the cake to cool in the bowl. Turn it out onto a cake plate and frost with buttercream frosting (page 48) tinted green. When sliced, people will enjoy having a piece of cake that looks just like a slice of watermelon, with its green and white rind and pink flesh with seeds.

English Birthday Cake

Birthdays, First/Last Days of School

In England, children's birthday cakes are usually only frosted between the layers and on the top. The sides are decorated with a strip of colored paper that has been folded and cut into a repetitive design—the way you make snowflakes and linked paper dolls. Sometimes gold or silver foil-covered paper is used. This makes a very pretty cake, and it has the added bonus of less frosting and less sugar.

Cupcakes, Muffins, and Ice Cream Treats

This section offers a plethora of useful recipes and ideas for kid pleasing snacks and special occasion treats. A cupcake tucked into a lunch box is always a welcomed surprise. A cupcake or muffin can make a perfect after school snack and makes portion control easy. And hot muffins, straight from the oven on a Sunday morning are a sure fire way to say, "I love you."

"You scream! I scream! We all scream for ice cream!" That old skip rope rhyme shows just how much a part of American culture ice cream is. Though not an American invention, ice cream remains the country's favorite companion to cake, particularly when used in the delicious combinations presented here.

Many times, the greatest pleasures in life come in small packages, and this section delivers page after page of testimony to that fact!

(Note: All the cupcake and muffin recipes in this section require standard muffin pans, with 2 1/2-inch cups, unless otherwise stated.)

Lunch Box Surprise Cupcakes

This excellent timesaver allows you to bake a variety of lunch box surprises from one batter. Start with the basic recipe and add your choice of ingredients to create several different treats.

Makes about 18

Cake:

1 (18 1/4-ounce) package white or devil's food cake mix

3 large eggs

1/3 cup vegetable oil

1 cup water

Buttercream frosting (optional; page 48)

Colored sprinkles or other cake decorations, to serve (optional)

Optional fillings:

Fruit preserves

Peanut butter and jelly

Instant pudding

Miniature peanut butter cups

Fruit pie fillings

Marshmallow cream

1. Preheat the oven to 350°F. Line muffin pans with paper baking cups and spray each one with nonstick cooking spray.

2. Combine the cake mix, eggs, oil, and water in a large bowl and blend with an electric mixer at medium speed for about 2 minutes.

3. Fill the prepared muffin cups halfway with batter. Then drop in the surprises of your choice, like small dollops of preserves or spoonfuls of instant pie filling. Put a teaspoon each of peanut butter and jelly into the cups for PB&J cupcakes or make other treasures by adding peanut butter cups. The batter will rise up around the filling.

4. Bake the cupcakes in the center of the oven for 15 to 20 minutes, until a toothpick inserted into the cake part comes out clean.

5. Let the cupcakes cool before frosting them with buttercream frosting. Top with additional decorations if desired. Arrange on a decorative plate and serve or store for a later use.

Handy Hint: For making cupcakes and muffins, a portion scoop (otherwise known as an ice cream scooper) is a handy tool to use for filling the cups.

Rocky Road Cupcakes

Those of you who have a passion for rocky road ice cream will love these cupcakes as well.
Chock-a-block with nuts, marshmallows, and chocolate chips, these delights will help any kid
down the rocky road from lunchtime to recess.

Makes about 18

1 (18 1/4-ounce) package devil's
food cake mix

3 large eggs

1/3 cup vegetable oil

1 cup water

1 cup miniature marshmallows

1 cup semisweet chocolate chips

1 cup chopped walnuts

Chocolate fudge frosting (page 48)

1. Preheat the oven to 350°F. Line muffin pans with paper baking cups and spray the cups with nonstick cooking spray.

2. Combine the cake mix, eggs, oil, and water in a large bowl and blend with an electric mixer at medium speed for about 2 minutes. Fold in the marshmallows, chocolate chips, and walnuts with a wooden spoon.

3. Fill the prepared muffin cups about two-thirds full with batter and bake in the center of the oven for 15 to 20 minutes, until a toothpick inserted into a cupcake center comes out clean.

4. Remove the cupcakes from the oven and cool completely before frosting. Arrange on a decorative plate and serve or store for a later use.

Ice Cream Cone Cakes

This is a delightful variation on the cupcake theme—one guaranteed to please any kid. The batter, scooped into flat-bottomed ice cream cones, can be baked plain or enhanced with M&M's candies, chocolate chips, small marshmallows, or nuts. After being baked, the tops can be decorated to look like ice cream cones.

Makes about 18

1 (18 1/4-ounce) package white or devil's food cake mix

3 large eggs

1/3 cup vegetable oil

1 cup water

About 18 flat-bottomed ice cream cones

Buttercream frosting or chocolate fudge frosting (page 48)

Optional ingredients:

M&M's candies

Small marshmallows

Chocolate chips

Chopped nuts

Crushed Heath bars

Crushed candy canes

Optional toppings:

Colored sprinkles

Coconut flakes, sweetened or unsweetened

Chocolate sprinkles

Chopped nuts

M&M's candies

1. Preheat the oven to 350°F.

2. Combine the cake mix, eggs, oil, and water in a large bowl and blend with an electric mixer at medium speed for about 2 minutes.

3. Fill the ice cream cones two-thirds full with batter and stand each one in the cup of a muffin pan.

4. If you are adding ingredients, scatter them on top of the batter and push them down into the batter with the end of a chopstick; make sure they are covered by batter. Make different cakes with as many different ingredients as you like.

5. Place the cones (in the muffin pans) in the center of the oven and bake for 15 to 20 minutes, until a toothpick inserted into a cake center comes out clean.

6. Remove the cones from the oven and allow to cool completely.

7. Frost the top of each cake-filled cone and decorate with your choice of toppings. Arrange the cupcakes on a decorative plate and serve or store for a later use.

Clown Cakes: Here is another fun idea that uses ice cream cones. Just bake your favorite cake mix in muffin pans that have been coated with nonstick cooking spray. Cool completely, then remove the cupcakes from the pans and frost with buttercream frosting (page 48). Stand a small conical wafer cone slightly askew on the top of the iced cupcake. Use flattened currants for the eyes, a small red hot candy for the nose, and pipe on a big smile with red frosting.

Liberty Cupcakes

Liberty cakes are perfect for glorious Fourth of July celebrations. Red, white, blue, and delicious, they are just the thing to start off any get-together with a bang! A variation follows.

Makes about 18

1 (18 1/4-ounce) package white cake mix

Red food coloring

Blue food coloring

Buttercream frosting (page 48)

Red and blue sprinkles, to serve

Cocktail picks with American flags, to serve (optional)

Cream Cupcakes: *Another sinfully delectable yet easy-to-make treat. First bake cupcakes as directed on the cake mix box. After they have cooled, remove from the baking dishes and slice off cupcake tops. With a spoon or melon baller, scoop out the center of the bottom half and fill with lightly sweetened whipped cream. Set the top back on and place the cupcakes on a wire rack placed over a jellyroll pan. Make a double recipe of the chocolate glaze (page 38-39) and pour it over the cakes. Let stand until the glaze sets. Then place each little cake on a small paper doily and serve.*

1. Line muffin pans with paper baking cups and spray the cups with nonstick cooking spray. Follow the manufacturer's directions for preparing the cake mix.

2. Divide the batter evenly into three small bowls. Use food coloring to tint one bowl red and one bowl blue and leave one bowl white.

3. Spoon some of each colored batter into the prepared muffin cups until they are two-thirds full. Bake as directed.

4. Remove the cupcakes from the oven and cool completely before decorating.

5. Decorating options:

   a. Frost the cupcake tops with white frosting and pipe thin concentric circles of red and blue frosting on top of the cakes. Draw a table knife or toothpick from the center to the outer edge in 5 or 6 places around the top of the cupcake. Draw the knife or toothpick in the opposite direction, between each line, from the outer edge inwards. The flower like effect is beautiful.

   b. Frost one-third of a cupcake top with red frosting, one-third with white frosting, and the remaining one-third with blue frosting.

   c. Frost the cupcake tops white and dust them with red and blue sprinkles or colored sugar.

   d. Once the cupcake tops are frosted, place small, paper star cutouts lightly on top of the frosting. Sprinkle the tops with red or blue sprinkles or colored sugar and carefully remove the paper. You will have stars where the paper stars were.

6. To serve, arrange the finished cupcakes on a decorative plate or store for a later use.

Black Bottom Cupcakes

Most black bottom cakes have chocolate pudding on the bottom. These little cakes get their black bottoms from a mixture of molasses, sugar, and currants. They can be a bit tricky to get out of the muffin pans, but they are well worth the extra fuss.

Makes about 18

1 1/2 cups of sugar

1/4 cup molasses

1/4 cup (1/2 stick) butter, softened

1/2 cup currants

1/2 teaspoon ground cinnamon

1/4 teaspoon ground nutmeg

1/4 teaspoon ground ginger

1 (18 1/4-ounce) package white cake mix

3 large eggs

1/3 cup vegetable oil

1 cup water

Warm baker's syrup (page 46)

1. Preheat the oven to 350°F. Line muffin pans with paper baking cups and spray the cups with nonstick cooking spray.

2. In a medium bowl, combine the sugar, molasses, butter, currants, cinnamon, nutmeg, and ginger and set aside.

3. Combine the cake mix, eggs, oil, and water in a large bowl and blend with an electric mixer at medium speed for about 2 minutes.

4. Divide the sugar-molasses mixture evenly between the muffin cups. Top with cake batter until the cups are about two-thirds full.

5. Bake the cupcakes in the center of the oven for 20 to 25 minutes, until a toothpick inserted into the centers comes out clean.

6. Remove the cupcakes from the oven and spoon a bit of baker's syrup over each. Cool completely.

7. To serve, carefully peel off the paper baking cups, place the cakes with their black bottoms up, then arrange on a serving plate.

St. Nicholas Cupcakes

These most special treats will gladden the heart of anybody at holiday time! They are also perfect for Santa's midnight snack. Kick off the holiday season on December 6, St. Nicholas Day, by serving these glazed, cranberry-filled gems to all your loved ones and friends.

Makes about 18

1 (18 1/4-ounce) package white cake mix

3 large eggs

1/3 cup vegetable oil

1 cup water

Whole cranberry sauce

Warm baker's syrup (page 46)

Small evergreen sprigs, to serve

Small candy canes, to serve

1. Preheat the oven to 350°F. Line muffin pans with paper baking cups and spray the cups with nonstick cooking spray.

2. Combine the cake mix, eggs, oil, and water in a large bowl and blend with an electric mixer at medium speed for about 2 minutes.

3. Fill the prepared muffin cups about two-thirds full with batter, then drop a teaspoon of the cranberry sauce in the center of each filled muffin cup.

4. Bake the cupcakes in the center of the oven for 20 to 25 minutes, until a toothpick inserted into a cupcake center comes out clean.

5. Immediately after you remove the cupcakes from the oven, paint the tops generously with baker's syrup and set aside to cool.

6. Pick over the evergreen sprigs and wash them under cold running water; shake dry. Unwrap the candy canes, then insert one along with a sprig of evergreen into the top of each cupcake. Arrange the finished cupcakes on a decorative plate and serve.

Fairy Cakes

Fairy cakes, a classic English teatime treat, are just very tiny cupcakes frosted in pastel tints. Sometimes the batter is tinted as well. Take the concept further by putting different flavorings in each of the different tinted batters—mint flavoring in tinted light green, lemon in yellow, cinnamon or peppermint in pink, etc.

Makes 48 to 72 (miniature size)

1 (18 1/4-ounce) package white cake mix

2 large eggs

1/4 cup (1/2 stick) butter, melted and cooled

1 cup water

Food coloring

Extract or flavoring of choice, such as mint, lemon, cinnamon, peppermint, almond, or vanilla (optional)

Buttercream frosting (page 48)

1. Preheat the oven to 350°F. Prepare miniature muffin pans with nonstick cooking spray.

2. Combine the cake mix, eggs, butter, and water into a large bowl and blend with an electric mixer at medium speed for about 2 minutes.

3. To tint and flavor the cakes, divide the batter into several small bowls and add just a drop of food coloring to each bowl to create pastel hues. Then add a few drops of flavoring to taste, if using.

4. Fill the cups of the miniature muffin pans two-thirds full with batter. Bake in the center of the oven for 12 to 15 minutes, until a toothpick inserted into the center of a cupcake comes out clean.

5. Remove the cupcakes from the oven and cool completely before removing them from the pans.

6. Use several more small bowls to tint the frosting as desired. Then frost the cupcakes and serve or store for a later use.

Handy Hint: If the recipe will make more Fairy Cakes than needed, use the remaining batter to make a few standard size cupcakes. For very special occasions, decorate the tops of each fairy cake with half a maraschino cherry, a bit of candied fruit peel, a crystallized edible flower (see page 75), or by piping on a simple design with a different colored frosting.

Madeleines

Here is a recipe for those lovely and expensive shell-shaped French cakes you find is fancy pastry shops. Just buy the appropriate baking dishes in a specialty cooking shop and you can make your own easily. In some parts of France, madeleines are served with a thin chocolate sauce and whipped cream.

Makes 96 to 108 (miniature size)

1 (18 1/4-ounce) package white cake mix

6 large eggs

1/4 cup (1/2 stick) butter, melted and cooled

1 tablespoon lemon or orange zest

1 teaspoon ground nutmeg

Orange-flavored liqueur, to taste (optional)

1. Preheat the oven to 350°F. Prepare the madeleine pans by spraying them with nonstick cooking spray.

2. Combine the cake mix, eggs, butter, zest, and nutmeg in a large bowl and blend at medium speed with an electric mixer for about 2 minutes.

3. Spoon the batter into the prepared pans and bake in the center of the oven for 8 to 10 minutes, until a toothpick inserted into the center of a cake comes out clean.

4. Remove the madeleines from the oven and sprinkle each generously with orange-flavored liqueur, if using. Allow to cool before turning out of the pans.

5. Remove the cakes from the pans, arrange on a pretty platter, and serve. They can also be stored in airtight containers for 2 or 3 weeks, but make sure they are completely cooled before storing or they will mold.

Handy Hint: If you don't wish to make so many madeleines, use the remaining batter for standard cupcakes or even a small cake.

Fresh Fruit Muffins

These muffins are best made in summer and autumn, when locally produced fruit is fresh, abundant, and at its best. Use soft fruits like cherries, peaches, apricots, or berries.

Makes about 18

1 (18 1/4-ounce) package white cake mix

3 large eggs

1/3 cup vegetable oil

3/4 cup water

1 1/2 cups diced fruit (preferably fresh)

About 2 cups streusel topping (optional; page 47)

Warm baker's syrup (page 46)

1. Preheat the oven to 375°F. Line muffin pans with paper baking cups and spray the cups with nonstick cooking spray.

2. Combine the cake mix, eggs, oil, and water in a large bowl and mix gently with a wooden spoon until all dry ingredients are moistened. Fold in the fruit.

3. Fill the prepared muffin cups two-thirds full with batter and top each with about 1 tablespoon of streusel topping, if using.

4. Bake the muffins in the center of the oven for 20 to 25 minutes, until a toothpick inserted into the center of a muffin comes out clean.

5. Remove the muffins from the oven and paint the tops liberally with baker's syrup. Allow them to cool for about 5 minutes before removing from the pans.

6. Transfer the muffins to a basket lined with a cloth and serve warm.

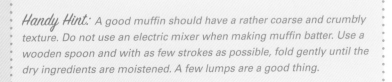

Handy Hint: A good muffin should have a rather coarse and crumbly texture. Do not use an electric mixer when making muffin batter. Use a wooden spoon and with as few strokes as possible, fold gently until the dry ingredients are moistened. A few lumps are a good thing.

Pumpkin-Spice Muffins

Serve these delicious spiced muffins for breakfast on a brisk autumn morning. When accompanied by sausages and fruit compote on Thanksgiving morning, your family will really rave.

Makes about 18

1 (18 1/4-ounce) package spice cake mix

3 large eggs

1/3 cup vegetable oil

1 cup water

1 teaspoon ground cinnamon

1/2 teaspoon ground nutmeg

1/2 teaspoon ground ginger

1/2 teaspoon allspice

1 cup canned pumpkin

About 2 cups streusel topping (page 47)

Warm baker's syrup (page 46)

1. Preheat the oven to 375°. Line muffin pans with paper baking cups and spray the cups with nonstick cooking spray.

2. Combine the cake mix, eggs, oil, water, cinnamon, nutmeg, ginger, allspice, and pumpkin in a large bowl and mix gently with a wooden spoon until all dry ingredients are moistened. Do not over mix.

3. Fill the prepared muffin cups about two-thirds full with batter. Top with about 1 tablespoon of streusel topping per muffin.

4. Bake the muffins in the center of the oven for 20 to 25 minutes, until a toothpick inserted into the center of a muffin comes out clean.

5. Spoon the warm baker's syrup over each muffin and allow them to sit in the muffin pans for about 5 minutes.

6. Place the muffins in a cloth-lined basket and serve warm.

All-Bran Raisin-Honey Muffins

Kellogg's introduced All-Bran cereal in the 1920s, and these muffins have been around ever since. Filling and delicious, it is the delightful pebbly texture and rich honey flavor that makes the recipe so timeless.

Makes about 24

1 (18 1/4-ounce) package spice cake mix

3 large eggs

1/3 cup vegetable oil

1/2 cup honey

2/3 cup water

2 cups bran cereal twigs, such as Kellogg's All-Bran

1 teaspoon ground cinnamon

1/2 teaspoon ground nutmeg

1/2 teaspoon ground ginger

1 cup dark raisins

Warm baker's syrup (page 46)

1. Preheat the oven to 375°F. Line muffin pans with paper baking cups and spray the cups with nonstick cooking spray.

2. Combine the cake mix, eggs, oil, honey, water, bran twigs, cinnamon, nutmeg, ginger, and raisins in a large bowl, then mix gently with a wooden spoon until all dry ingredients are moistened.

3. Fill the prepared muffin cups about two-thirds full with batter. Bake in the center of the oven for 20 to 24 minutes, until a toothpick inserted into the center of a muffin comes out clean.

4. Remove the muffins from the oven and paint generously with baker's syrup. Allow them to cool for about 5 minutes before removing from the pans.

5. Place the muffins in a cloth-lined basket and serve warm.

Handy Hint: If you don't have enough batter to fill all of the cups in your muffin pans when baking cupcakes or muffins, fill the empty cups halfway with water. This will aid in even baking, and it will keep your pans from warping.

Oatmeal Molasses Muffins

Talk about old-fashioned breakfast fun! These spiced oatmeal treats conjure images of winter mornings in Grandma's warm kitchen, where a batch of fragrant, warm muffins were delivered to the table straight from the oven. Serve with homemade jam or preserves for extra flavor. Five variations follow.

Makes about 18

1 (18 1/4-ounce) package spice cake mix

3 large eggs

1/3 cup vegetable oil

1/3 cup molasses

1 cup water

2 cups quick-cooking oats

About 2 cups streusel topping (page 47)

Warm baker's syrup (page 46)

1. Preheat the oven to 375°F. Line muffin pans with paper baking cups and spray the cups with nonstick cooking spray.

2. Combine the cake mix, eggs, oil, molasses, water, and oats in a large bowl and mix gently with a wooden spoon until all dry ingredients are moistened.

3. Fill the prepared muffin cups about one-third full with batter. Top with about 1 tablespoon of streusel topping per muffin.

4. Bake in the center of the oven for 20 to 25 minutes, until a toothpick inserted into a muffin center comes out clean.

5. Remove the muffins from the oven and paint each one liberally with baker's syrup. Cool for about 5 minutes before removing the muffins from the pans and placing them in a cloth-lined basket. Serve warm.

Carrot Muffins: *Replace the oats in Oatmeal Molasses Muffins with 2 cups grated carrot. Complete the recipe as directed.*

Apple Cinnamon Muffins: *Replace the oats in Oatmeal Molasses Muffins with 2 cups peeled, cored, and chopped apples and 1 tablespoon ground cinnamon. Complete the recipe as directed.*

Granola Muffins: *Replace the oats in Oatmeal Molasses Muffins with 2 cups granola. Complete the recipe as directed.*

Raisin Nut Muffins: *Replace the oats in Oatmeal Molasses Muffins with 1 cup raisins and 1 cup chopped walnuts. Complete recipe as directed.*

Tropical Sun Muffins: *Replace the oats in Oatmeal Molasses Muffins with 1/2 cup coconut flakes, 1/2 cup chopped dried pineapple, 1/2 cup chopped dried papaya, and 1/2 cup chopped macadamia nuts. Complete the recipe as directed.*

Mint-Chip Ice Cream Loaf

Served in slices on chilled plates, this beautiful frozen creation doubles as both an elegant ending to any meal and a self-indulgent treat anytime. It is best to bake the cake the day before assembling the loaf. You also want the ice cream to be as hard as possible. This is an excellent dessert for St. Patrick's Day.

Serves 10 to 12

1 (18 1/4-ounce) package devil's food cake mix

2 large eggs

1/3 cup vegetable oil

1 cup water

1 (1/2-gallon) block mint chocolate chip ice cream

Handy Hint: If you can't find block ice cream, line a freezer-proof loaf pan with parchment paper, allowing several inches to hang over the sides. Fill the pan with ice cream and freeze solid. When ready to assemble the loaf, you will be able to remove the ice cream from the pan by pulling on the overhanging paper.

1. Preheat the oven to 350°F. Prepare a 9 x 5-inch loaf pan.

2. Combine the cake mix, eggs, oil, and water in a large bowl and blend with an electric mixer at medium speed for about 2 minutes.

3. Pour the batter into the prepared pan and bake in the center of the oven for 30 to 35 minutes, until a toothpick inserted into the center comes out clean. Cool completely.

4. Remove the cake from the pan and trim the top to be level. Lay the loaf on its side and cut it into 1/2-inch slices lengthwise.

5. Working quickly, remove the ice cream from its container and trim it into a block the same size as the cake before slicing. Slice the block of ice cream into 1/2-inch slices. Sometimes this is made easier by running the knife under hot water between each slice.

6. Put a slice of cake on a large piece of plastic wrap or parchment paper. Lay a slice of ice cream on top, and then place another slice of cake on top of the ice cream. Continue with this pattern until you have assembled all the layers of cake and ice cream, ending with cake as the top slice. Wrap the entire loaf in plastic wrap and return to the freezer until ready to serve.

7. Unwrap the ice cream loaf, then cut it into slices about 3/4-inch thick. Serve on chilled plates.

Frozen Fudge Dream Cupcakes

This frozen delight is a chocoholic's dream: devil's food cake surrounding a fudge ice cream core amongst pools of chocolate syrup and clouds of fresh whipped cream. If possible, make the cupcakes the day before for easier assembly.

Makes about 18

1 (18 1/4-ounce) package devil's food cake mix

3 large eggs

1/3 cup vegetable oil

2 ounces (2 squares) baker's chocolate, chopped and melted

1 cup strong-brewed coffee, cold

Chocolate fudge ice cream

Whipped cream, lightly sweetened, to serve

Chocolate syrup, to serve

Finely chopped walnuts or shaved chocolate, to serve

1. Preheat the oven to 350°F. Line muffin pans with paper baking cups and spray the cups with nonstick cooking spray.

2. Combine the cake mix, eggs, oil, melted chocolate, and coffee in a large bowl and blend with an electric mixer at medium speed for about 2 minutes.

3. Fill the prepared muffin cups about two-thirds full with batter and bake in the center of the oven for 20 to 25 minutes, until a toothpick inserted into the center of a cupcake comes out clean. Remove from the oven and cool completely.

4. Slice the top off of each cupcake. With a spoon or melon baller, scoop out the inside of the cupcake, creating a little cake bowl. Working quickly, put a scoop of ice cream inside each cake and set the top back on. Wrap each filled cake in plastic wrap and return it to the freezer for at least an hour before serving.

5. To serve, unwrap the cupcakes and set each on a dessert plate. Top each with whipping cream and a generous drizzle of chocolate syrup. Sprinkle with chopped nuts, if desired.

Chocolate-Orange Ice Cream Cake

Nothing says Halloween like black and orange and treats! This sweet creation is ideal for that end-of-October party, layering spiced pumpkin cake with rich chocolate ice cream. Bake the cake the day before, if possible, and assemble the layers in advance or store the cake for several days before assembling.

Serves 10 to 12

1 (18 1/4-ounce) package spice cake mix

2 large eggs

1/3 cup vegetable oil

1 cup canned pumpkin

1 cup water

Orange food coloring

1 quart chocolate ice cream

Whipped cream, to serve (optional)

Chocolate sprinkles, to serve (optional)

1. Preheat the oven to 350°F. Prepare a 10-inch springform pan.

2. Combine the cake mix, eggs, oil, pumpkin, and water in a large bowl and blend with an electric mixer at medium speed for about 2 minutes. Add enough orange food coloring to make a bright orange batter. Mix thoroughly.

3. Pour the batter into the prepared pan and bake in the center of the oven for 35 to 40 minutes, until a toothpick inserted into the center comes out clean. Cool the cake completely before removing it from the pan.

4. Remove the ice cream from the freezer and allow it to soften slightly. Do not allow to melt.

5. Meanwhile, remove the cake from its pan and trim the top to produce a flat surface. Split the cake horizontally into two even layers. Dust off all the excess crumbs.

6. Place one cake layer in the bottom of a clean 10-inch springform pan. In a large bowl, whip the softened ice cream with a large spoon until it is malleable. Spread an even layer of ice cream about 1-inch thick over the top of the cake. Put the second layer of cake on top of the ice cream. Fill the pan with the remaining ice cream, smooth the top, cover with plastic wrap, and return to the freezer until the ice cream has set.

7. If you are going to frost the cake with whipped cream, prepare the whipped cream before removing the cake from the freezer. When ready, work quickly to remove the sides of the pan. (Note: Running a knife around the edge is best.) With two spatulas or bench knives, loosen the cake from the pan and carefully transfer it to a chilled serving plate. Frost the top with the whipped cream and sprinkle with chocolate sprinkles, if using.

8. Slice the cake and serve on chilled plates.

Mini Baked Alaskas

This scrumptious dessert is a bit of a fiddle to make, but it is well worth the trouble. You may make it with a white or chocolate cake mix and chocolate or vanilla ice cream—whatever combination you wish. You may also bake the cake the day before if preferred.

Makes about 12

1 (18 1/4-ounce) package white or devil's food cake mix

4 large eggs, separated

1/3 cup vegetable oil

1 1/3 cup water

1 quart vanilla or chocolate ice cream

1/4 cup sugar

1 tablespoon vanilla extract

1. Preheat the oven to 350°F. Line a standard jelly roll pan with parchment paper.

2. Combine the cake mix, 4 egg yolks, oil, and water in a large bowl and blend with an electric mixer at medium speed for about 2 minutes.

3. Pour the batter into the prepared pan and spread evenly. Bake in the center of the oven for 20 to 25 minutes, until a toothpick inserted into the center comes out clean.

4. Remove the cake from the oven and allow it to cool completely before turning it out of the pan.

5. When cool, quickly invert the pan onto a flat surface. Carefully peel off the parchment paper. With a 2 1/2- or 3-inch round cutter, cut the cake into rounds. Dust off all the loose crumbs and place on a clean baking sheet lined with more parchment paper.

6. Top each round of cake with a symmetrical scoop of ice cream, then put the pan in the freezer and leave until just before you wish to serve. The ice cream should be very firm.

7. Beat the 4 egg whites in a medium bowl with an electric mixer until soft peaks form. Slowly add the sugar and vanilla extract and continue to beat until firm peaks hold.

8. Turn the broiler setting to high, or if you do not have a broiler setting, turn your oven to the highest mark and preheat.

9. Remove the ice cream cakes from the freezer and move quickly to frost them completely with the egg white meringue. Place the pan under the broiler in the center of the oven and leave only for about 1 minute, just until the meringue begins to brown. The trick is to brown the meringue before the ice cream melts. If you have a kitchen blowtorch, use it instead of the oven. Serve on chilled plates.

Handy Hint: Egg whites will not stiffen if there is any oil or fat of any kind. Make sure there is absolutely no yolk in with the whites. Always wash your bowl and beaters with detergent and hot water just before beating egg whites to make sure no airborne cooking oils have accumulated on them.

Ice Cream Sandwiches

The beauty of many homemade ice cream snacks is that you can make them ahead of time and enjoy them at your convenience. These classic frozen sandwiches, for example, are easily prepared in advance and keep well in the freezer when wrapped in plastic wrap. Six suggestions for cookie-ice cream combinations follow.

Make as many or as few as you wish

Ice cream of choice

Cookies of choice (page 77-83)

Suggested combinations:

Vanilla cookies and chocolate swirl ice cream

Vanilla cookies and butter brickle, pecan praline, or similar ice cream

Vanilla cookies and peach, berry, or other fruit ice cream

Chocolate cookies and vanilla ice cream

Chocolate cookies and mint chocolate chip ice cream

Chocolate cookies and coffee ice cream

1. Remove the ice cream from the freezer and allow it to soften slightly. Do not allow to melt.

2. Meanwhile, line a jelly roll pan with parchment paper. In a large bowl, whip the softened ice cream with a large spoon or fork until it is malleable.

3. Spread the ice cream in an even 1/2-inch-thick layer in the pan, then freeze until firm.

4. Remove the ice cream from the freezer and, working quickly, turn it out of the pan onto a flat surface. Peel off the parchment paper. Using a round cutter approximately the same size as the cookies, cut the ice cream into rounds.

5. Sandwich each round of ice cream between two cookies, wrap each sandwich in a piece of plastic wrap or aluminum foil, and keep in the freezer until serving.

Frozen Fool

In England, a traditional fool is a dessert made by folding crushed fresh fruit into firmly whipped cream. It gets its name because it is so easy to make, even a fool can do it. For this delicious version, instead of using fruit, use cake crumbs made from leftover cake or the scraps of cake left from slicing off the tops to make them even.

Serves 6 to 8

1/2 pint heavy cream

1 tablespoon sugar, or to taste

1 tablespoon liqueur of choice

2 cups cake crumbs

2 crushed Heath Toffee Bars (optional)

1. In a medium bowl, whip the cream into soft peaks. Sprinkle the sugar over the top, add the liqueur, and continue whipping until it holds firm peaks. Fold in the cake crumbs and crushed candy bars, if using.

2. Spoon the mixture into tall serving glasses and chill for at least an hour before serving.

Crystallized Flowers and Leaves

Here's an easy recipe for elegantly decorating cakes and cupcakes. Note: This recipe contains raw eggs.

1 large egg white

1 tablespoon water

Small flowers and/or leaves of choice, such as miniature roses, rose petals, violets, violas,

Pansies, borage blossoms, or mint leaves

Sugar

1. Put the egg white and water in a small bowl and whip lightly with a fork. Allow to sit until the foam has subsided.

2. Meanwhile, gently rinse the flowers in cold water, remove the stems, and set aside to dry.

3. Fill a small, shallow plate with sugar.

4. When the flowers are dry, use a clean soft brush to paint one side of a blossom with egg white, then sprinkle with the sugar. Lay each blossom on waxed paper and set aside to dry.

5. When dry, repeat the process on the other side of the flowers, giving them time to air dry. Do not try to speed up the process by placing the flowers in an oven; this will turn them brown. Once the blossoms are completely dry, use them to decorate cupcakes and other pastries. They can be stored in airtight containers for several months.

Cookies and Bars

Many of the joys of childhood have vanished from the American scene. Jacks, hop-scotch, jump rope, marbles, kick the can, and hide and seek have stepped aside to make way for T.V., video games, and rollerblades. One traditional icon of childhood remains; the well filled cookie jar. Keeping that cookie jar filled need not be the tedious and time consuming effort it use to be. With the recipes in this section you do not need to be a stay-at-home mom to produce these sure fire kid pleasers. Better yet, make keeping the cookie jar full a family affair.

Peanut Butter Cookies

With its distinctive crosshatch design, this cookie and a glass of milk are as healing to the soul as chicken soup is to the body. In fact, peanut butter cookies offer a great reason to stay home and play hookie for a day!

Makes about 36

1 (18 1/4-ounce) package white
  cake mix

2 large eggs

2 cups chunky style peanut butter

1. Preheat the oven to 375°F. Line baking sheets with parchment paper.

2. Combine the cake mix and eggs in a large bowl and blend well with an electric mixer at medium speed for two minutes. Add the peanut butter and fold in using a large wooden spoon until thoroughly incorporated.

3. Use a portion scoop or tablespoon to make balls of dough. Place the balls on the baking sheets about 1 1/2 to 2 inches apart.

4. Spray the bottom of a glass with nonstick cooking spray and flatten each ball to be about 1/2-inch thick. Spray the back of a fork or dip in a bit of oil and press gently on the top of each cookie to make crosshatch marks on the top.

5. Bake the cookies in the center of the oven for 15 to 20 minutes, until the edges just start to brown. Serve warm or cool completely for storage.

Plain Drop Cookies

A drop cookie is simple and delicious just as is, though it is used as the beginning for a myriad of other creations, such as cream and ice cream sandwiches and that all time favorite—Snickerdoodles! Five variations follow.

Makes about 36

1 (18 1/4-ounce) package cake mix of choice (preferably white, spice, or devil's food)

3 large eggs

1/3 cup vegetable oil

Extract or flavoring of choice, to taste (vanilla, lemon zest, almond extract, spices, etc.)

1. Preheat the oven to 375°F. Line baking sheets with parchment paper.

2. Combine the cake mix, eggs, oil, and flavoring in a large bowl and blend well with an electric mixer at medium speed for two minutes.

3. Use a portion scoop or tablespoon to make balls of dough. Place the balls about 1 1/2 inches apart on the baking sheets, then spray the bottom of a glass with nonstick cooking spray. Use the glass to flatten each ball into rounds less than 1/2-inch thick.

4. Bake for 15 to 20 minutes, depending on the texture desired. (Some people like them quite crisp, while others prefer them on the chewy side.)

5. Allow the cookies to cool on the baking sheet or transfer them to a tray for cooling. Serve or store for a later use. (Note: Cookies should be completely cool before storing.)

Handy Hints: For making drop cookies, portion scoopers are a good idea. They usually cost from $9.00 to $16.00 and are available in specialty stores and online. Each manufacturer seems to have a different sizing system. For most drop cookies, use one that holds about 1 level tablespoon, and for muffins, about 3 tablespoons.

Snickerdoodles: *Before placing the Plain Drop Cookies on the baking sheet and flattening them, roll the balls of dough in a mixture of 1 cup sugar with 1 tablespoon ground cinnamon. Complete the recipe as directed.*

Cream Sandwiches: *Bake the cookies as directed for Plain Drop Cookies, allowing adequate time for cooling. Make buttercream frosting (page 48) or chocolate fudge frosting (page 48). Spread frosting on the baked cookies and top each with a second cookie.*

PB&J Cookie Sandwiches: *Bake the cookies as directed for Plain Drop Cookies, allowing adequate time for cooling. Spread the baked cookies with peanut butter and jelly and top each with a second cookie.*

Fluffernutter Cookie Sandwiches: *Bake the cookies as directed for Plain Drop Cookies, allowing adequate time for cooling. Spread crunchy peanut butter and marshmallow cream onto baked cookies. Top each with a second cookie.*

S'more Cookies: *Bake the cookies as directed for Plain Drop Cookies, allowing adequate time for cooling. Top each of the baked cookies with a square of chocolate bar. Top that with a marshmallow, then arrange the cookies on a baking sheet. Set the broiler to medium and put the baking sheet under it for 30 seconds to 1 minute, until the marshmallow just begins to puff and brown. Top with a second cookie and serve immediately.*

P-Nutty-O's

This is most definitely a kid's cookie, combining everything a kid loves: peanuts, Cheerios, peanut butter, and cookies. Crunchy, soft, sweet, and salty—what more could any of us want?

Makes about 36

1 (18 1/4-ounce) package spice cake mix

2 large eggs

1/3 cup vegetable oil

1 cup chunky peanut butter

1 cup roasted peanuts

1 cup toasted oat cereal, such as Cheerios

Warm baker's syrup (page 46)

1. Preheat the oven to 375°F. Line baking sheets with parchment paper.

2. Combine the cake mix, eggs, and oil in a large bowl and blend with an electric mixer at medium speed for two minutes. Add the peanut butter, peanuts, and cereal and fold in using a large wooden spoon until incorporated.

3. Drop rounded tablespoons of dough onto the lined baking sheets, leaving about 2 inches between each cookie. Flatten slightly with fingers tips.

4. Bake the cookies in the center of the oven for 15 to 20 minutes, until golden brown.

5. Once the cookies are removed from the oven, paint them liberally with baker's syrup. Serve warm or cool completely for storage.

Chocolate Chip Cookies

Chocolate chip cookies of one sort or another have been around since the 1930s, the tasty result of a mishap in the kitchen of the Toll House Inn outside of Boston. They have remained a classic favorite ever since.

Makes about 48

1 (18 1/4-ounce) package spice cake mix

3 large eggs

1/3 cup vegetable oil

1 tablespoon molasses

2 cups (one 12-ounce package) semisweet chocolate chips

1 cup chopped walnuts

1. Preheat the oven to 375°F. Line baking sheets with parchment paper.

2. Combine the cake mix, eggs, oil, and molasses in a large bowl and blend well with a wooden spoon. Add the chocolate chips and walnuts and stir until incorporated.

3. Drop rounded tablespoons of dough onto the lined baking sheets, leaving about 2 inches between each cookie.

4. Bake in center of the oven for 12 to 15 minutes, until golden brown. Serve warm or cool completely for storage.

Handy Hints: If your cookies turn out crisper than you like, put them in your cookie jar or other container with 1/2 an apple for a day or two. They will absorb the moisture from the apple and soften a bit.

The Ultimate Drop Cookie

This is the Ultimate Drop Cookie, combining everything good in one spectacular cookie. The recipe makes a lot of cookies, as they will vanish quickly.

Makes about 60

1 (18 1/4-ounce) package spice cake mix

3 large eggs

1/3 cup vegetable oil

1 cup chopped walnuts

1 cup quick-cooking oats

1 cup dark raisins

1 cup semisweet chocolate chips

Milk, as needed

Warm baker's syrup (page 46)

1. Preheat the oven to 375°F. Line baking sheets with parchment paper.

2. Combine the cake mix, eggs, and oil in a large bowl and blend well with a wooden spoon. Add the walnuts, oats, raisins, and chocolate chips and continue to stir until all are incorporated. You may need to add a tablespoon or two of milk if the dough is difficult to work with. It should be stiff but malleable.

3. Drop rounded tablespoons of dough onto the lined baking sheets, leaving about 2 inches between each cookie. Flatten the dough slightly with the back of a wooden spoon.

4. Bake in the center of the oven for 15 to 20 minutes, until golden brown.

5. Remove the cookies from the oven and paint them generously with baker's syrup while they are still hot. Serve warm or cool completely for storage.

Coconut Drops

These delectable little drop cookies are very close to macaroons. Light and airy, yet chewy, they are a perfect teatime treat.

Makes about 36

1 (18 1/4-ounce) package white cake mix

4 large egg whites, lightly beaten

1/3 cup vegetable oil

3 cups coconut flakes, sweetened or unsweetened

1 tablespoon almond extract

1. Preheat the oven to 350°F. Line baking sheets with parchment paper.

2. Combine the cake mix, egg whites, oil, coconut, and almond extract in a large bowl and blend well with a wooden spoon.

3. Drop rounded tablespoons of dough onto the lined baking sheets, leaving about 1 1/2 inches between each cookie.

4. Bake in the center of the oven for about 20 minutes or until lightly golden brown. Remove from the oven and allow to cool before serving or storing.

Thumbprint Cookies

Fill the thumb depression in these cookies with kid-friendly jam or jelly or a dollop of peanut butter and a dollop of jelly. For adults, try a dab of softened cream cheese and a dab of wine jelly, or for the truly sophisticated use red, yellow, and green pepper jam or jelly. Five variations follow.

Makes about 36

1 (18 1/4-ounce) package white cake mix

3/4 cup all-purpose flour

1/3 cup cornstarch

1/2 cup (1 stick) butter, cut into small pieces

1 large egg

1 tablespoon vanilla extract

1 tablespoon water

About 2 cups finely chopped peanuts, walnuts, almonds, or pecans

Filling(s) of choice, such as jam, jelly, peanut butter, cream cheese, etc.

1. Preheat the oven to 375°F. Line baking sheets with parchment paper.

2. Combine the cake mix, flour, and cornstarch in a large bowl and toss to mix well. Add the butter, egg, vanilla extract, and water and blend until you have a soft dough. You may find that your hands are the best tool. Set aside.

3. Put the nuts into a shallow bowl.

4. Scoop up about 1 tablespoon of dough at a time and roll into a ball. Roll the balls in the nuts to coat evenly, then place the balls about 2 inches apart on the baking sheets. Lightly flour your thumb and press gently on each ball of dough to make an indent.

5. Bake in the center of the oven for about 12 to 15 minutes, until they are golden brown.

6. Cool completely before filling the indentations with your choice of filling. Arrange on a plate and serve.

Russian Tea Cakes: Make Thumbprint Cookies but add 1 cup of very finely chopped walnuts to the dough. Proceed as directed but leave in round balls for baking. Remove the cookies from the oven and as soon as they are cool enough to touch, place them in a small paper bag with a cup of confectioners' sugar and shake gently. Set aside to cool before serving.

Welsh Tea Cakes: Make Thumbprint Cookies but leave the dough in round balls for baking. Remove the cookies from the oven and, as soon as they are cool enough to touch, place them in a small paper bag with a cup of confectioners' sugar and shake gently. Set aside to cool before serving.

Ma-Ma-Mamools (Arabic): Make Thumbprint Cookies but replace the vanilla and water with 2 tablespoons of lemon juice. Add 1 tablespoon of lemon zest to the dough as well. Leave the dough in round balls for baking. Remove the cookies from the oven and, as soon as they are cool enough to touch, place them in a small paper bag with a cup of confectioners' sugar and shake gently. Set aside to cool before serving.

Pfeffernusse (German Christmas Cakes): Make Thumbprint Cookies but add 1 cup of very finely chopped walnuts, 1/2 cup very finely minced fruitcake mix, and 1/2 teaspoon fine ground black pepper to the dough. Proceed as directed but leave in round balls for baking. Remove the cookies from the oven and as soon as they are cool enough to touch, place them in a small paper bag with a cup of confectioners' sugar and 1 teaspoon ground nutmeg, shake gently. Set aside to cool before serving.

Mexican Wedding Cakes: Make Thumbprint Cookies but add 1 teaspoon ground cinnamon to the dough. Leave the dough in round balls for baking. Remove the cookies from the oven and, as soon as they are cool enough to touch, place them in a small paper bag with a cup of confectioners' sugar, 2 tablespoons powdered cocoa, and 1 teaspoon ground cinnamon, shake gently. Set aside to cool before serving.

Solstice Cakes

This shortbread-like cookie has Scottish origins. It was traditionally baked on the winter solstice (the shortest day of the year) in round cakes, fluted around the edges to represent the sun. It was hoped that it would entice the return of the waning sun. A variation follows.

Makes 24 to 32

1 (18 1/4-ounce) package white cake mix

1 teaspoon ground nutmeg

3/4 cup (1 1/2 sticks) butter, cut into small pieces

Raw, turbinado, or Demerara sugar

1. Preheat the oven to 325°F. Assemble two, 7 1/2- to 8-inch quiche pans with removable bottoms.

2. Combine the cake mix and nutmeg in a large bowl and toss to mix well.

3. Add the small pieces of butter, and with a wire pastry blender or your hands, mix as you would piecrust, until the butter is thoroughly incorporated and the texture is that of coarse cornmeal.

4. Divide the mixture between the two quiche pans and press the dough with the palms of your hands to flatten, smooth, and press into the fluted edges of the pans. Sprinkle the top of each pan with raw sugar and press into the dough.

5. Bake in the center of the oven for about 40 to 45 minutes, until the top is a pale buff color. You do not want it to brown. Remove from the oven and while the dough is still hot, use a small, slim bladed knife and cut each pan into 12 or 16 equal pie-shaped wedges. Allow to cool completely before removing from the pans. Don't worry if some of the wedges break when you remove them. This cookie is best if stored in an airtight container for at least a week before serving.

Handy Hint: It is easier to get even pieces if you cut each pan into equal quarters first, then cut each quarter into 3 or 4 equal wedges.

Le Gâteau du Soleil "The cake of the sun": This almond enhanced French version of the Solstice Cake comes from the ancient southern French walled city of Carcassonne. Replace the nutmeg with 1 teaspoon almond extract. Before baking, paint the tops of each pan with an egg white lightly beaten with 1 tablespoon of water, and scatter finely sliced blanched almonds on the top. Bake as directed above. Traditionally it is not cut but left whole for people to break off pieces of it.

Rolled Cookies

Rolled cookies are an absolute must for holidays and special occasions. They are so popular that there are cookie cutter collectors clubs where some people own thousands.

Makes 24 to 36 (depending on cutter size)

1 (18 1/4-ounce) package white cake mix

1 cup all-purpose flour

2 large eggs

1/4 cup vegetable oil

1 teaspoon vanilla extract

Buttercream frosting (page 48)

1. Preheat the oven to 375°F. Line baking sheets with parchment paper.

2. Combine the cake mix, flour, eggs, oil, and vanilla extract in a large bowl and blend well with a wooden spoon. Turn the dough out onto a lightly floured surface and knead just enough to pull all the dough together into a ball. Divide the dough into quarters. Set one quarter on the lightly floured surface and put the other three back into the bowl and cover with plastic wrap to keep from drying out.

3. Form the quarter into a ball and flatten into a disk about 1/2-inch thick. Make sure there is a dusting of flour under the dough. Lightly dust the top of the disk and with a rolling pin roll into a circle about 1/4-inch thick. Give the sheet of dough a quarter turn now and then as you roll to keep it evenly round and prevent sticking.

4. Put a little pile of flour to one side of your work area and dip your cutters in this before using to shape your cookies. With a spatula or bench knife, lift the cookies onto the lined baking sheets leaving about 2 inches between each cookie.

5. Gather up the scraps of dough and add them to one of the pieces of dough in the bowl, knead gently and form into a ball, flatten, roll, and cut as before. Repeat the process until all cookies have been formed.

6. Bake in the center of the oven for 12 to 15 minutes, until they are a pale golden brown. Remove them from the baking sheet with a spatula and allow to cool on a tray or on a sheet of parchment paper.

7. Use buttercream frosting tinted several different colors to decorate the cookies. Let your creativity and your imagination be your guide.

Gingerbread Men

*Gingerbread Men cookies are as much a part of a traditional and old fashion Christmas as the
Christmas tree, roast goose, and chestnuts roasting on an open fire.*

Makes 24 to 36 (depending on cutter size)

1 (18 1/4-ounce) package spice
  cake mix

1 cup all-purpose flour

2 large eggs

1/4 cup vegetable oil

1/4 cup dark molasses

1 tablespoon ground cinnamon

1 tablespoon ground ginger

Buttercream frosting (page 48)

1. Preheat the oven to 350°F. Line baking sheets with parchment paper.

2. Combine the cake mix, flour, eggs, oil, molasses, cinnamon, and
ginger in a large bowl and blend well with a wooden spoon. Turn the
dough out onto a lightly floured surface and knead just enough to pull
all the dough together into a ball. Divide the dough into quarters. Set
one quarter on the lightly floured surface and put the other three back
into the bowl and cover with plastic wrap to keep from drying out.

3. Form the quarter into a ball and flatten into a disk about 1/2-inch
thick. Be sure there is a dusting of flour under the dough. Lightly dust
the top of the disk and with a rolling pin roll into a circle that is about
1/4-inch thick. Give the sheet of dough a quarter turn now and then as
you roll to keep it evenly round and prevent sticking.

4. Put a little pile of flour to one side of your work area and dip your
cutters in this before using to shape your cookies. With a spatula or
bench knife, lift the cookies onto the lined baking sheets leaving
about 2 inches between each cookie.

5. Gather up the scraps of dough and add them to one of the pieces
of dough in the bowl, form into a ball and repeat the process until all
cookies have been formed.

6. Bake in the center of the oven for 12 to 15 minutes, until they are
golden brown. Remove them from the baking sheet with a spatula and
allow to cool on a tray or on a sheet of parchment paper.

7. When the gingerbread men are completely cool, use buttercream
frosting to pipe on faces or the names of the people you are going to
give them to.

Dream Cakes

Just imagine squares of a shortbread-like cookie topped with chocolate and nuts. For chocolate lovers, these old-fashioned bars are a glorious waking dream.

Makes about 36

Solstice Cakes (page 86)

1 cup chopped walnuts

1 (12-ounce) package semisweet chocolate chips

1. Line a 9 x 13-inch baking dish with parchment paper.

2. Prepare the dough for Solstice Cakes, then press into the prepared pan. Bake as directed.

3. Scatter the nuts and chocolate chips over the top of the bars while they are still warm.

4. Turn the oven up to 400°F, return the bars to the oven when preheating is complete, and leave them in there only until the chocolate chips have melted, 2 to 3 minutes.

5. Cut the bars into squares while still warm and serve at once or wait until they have cooled to room temperature.

Honey-Nut Bars

These delicious bars, chock-full with honey, spices, and nuts are sure to please kids and grown-ups.
Three variations follow.

Makes about 36

1 (18 1/4-ounce) package spice cake mix

1 tablespoon ground cinnamon

1 teaspoon ground nutmeg

1/2 teaspoon ground ginger

1/2 teaspoon allspice

3 large eggs

1/3 cup vegetable oil

1 cup honey

1 cup plus 2 tablespoons water

1 cup coarsely chopped walnuts

About 1/2 cup ground walnuts

1. Preheat the oven to 350°F. Prepare one 9 x 13-inch or two 8 x 8-inch baking dishes.

2. Combine the cake mix, cinnamon, nutmeg, ginger, and allspice in a large bowl and toss together to mix thoroughly.

3. Add the eggs, oil, 1/2 cup honey, and 1 cup water and blend with an electric mixer for about 2 minutes. Fold in the chopped nuts with a wooden spoon.

4. Pour the batter into the prepared dish and bake in the center of the oven for 30 to 35 minutes, until a toothpick inserted in the center comes out clean.

5. While the pans are in the oven, heat the other 1/2 cup of honey with the 2 tablespoons of water until the honey is melted and blended with the water.

6. As soon as the pans come out of the oven, pour the honey mixture over them. Sprinkle on the ground nuts and allow to cool completely.

7. When cooled, a 9 x 13-inch pan can be cut into approximately 36 bars and each 8 x 8-inch pan can be cut into 16 bars. They store very well.

Holiday Fruit Bars: *Follow the Honey-Nut Bars recipe, but add 1 cup of chopped candied fruitcake mix along with the chopped nuts. Bake as directed. Substitute about 1/2 cup of baker's syrup (page 46) for the honey to be poured over the top. The topping of ground nuts is optional.*

Grandma's Molasses-Nut Swirls: *Follow the Honey-Nut Bars recipe, but substitute 1/3 cup of molasses for the half cup of honey. After pouring the batter into the prepared pans, drizzle about 1/2 cup of molasses over the top. Don't try and spread it evenly. You want to find pockets of it when you bite into the finished bars. Bake as directed.*

Date-Nut Bars: *Follow the Honey-Nut Bars recipe, but add 1 cup pitted and chopped dates in addition to the chopped nuts. Bake as directed. Omit the topping of honey and nuts. Instead, after the bars have been cut, roll them gently in confectioners' sugar.*

Blondies

For white chocolate lovers, this is a dream come true. These bars are moist, rich, and just dripping with white chocolate.

Makes about 36

1 (18 1/4-ounce) package white cake mix

3 large eggs

1/3 cup vegetable oil

1 cup sour cream

2 ounces (2 squares) white chocolate, chopped and melted

1 (12-ounce) package white chocolate chips

1 cup chopped blanched almonds (optional)

Whipped cream (optional)

1. Preheat the oven to 350°F. Prepare a 9 x 13-inch baking dish.

2. Combine the cake mix, eggs, oil, sour cream, and melted chocolate in a large bowl and blend with an electric mixer at medium speed for about 2 minutes. Fold in the chocolate chips and almonds with a wooden spoon.

3. Pour the batter into the prepared dish and bake in the center of the oven for 30 to 35 minutes, until a toothpick inserted into the center comes out clean.

4. Cool the bars before turning them out of the pan and cutting into squares. Serve as is or with a dollop of whipped cream, if desired.

Espresso Bars

If you like chocolate and coffee, this creation is just the thing for you. With all the caffeine in the coffee and chocolate, they make an excellent pick-me-up in the afternoon. They are most definitely an adult indulgence.

Makes 32

1 (18 1/4-ounce) package devil's food cake mix

1/3 cup vegetable oil

4 large eggs

1 cup plus 2/3 cup strong-brewed dark roast coffee, cold

2 ounces (2 squares) baker's chocolate, chopped and melted

2 tablespoons ground dark roast coffee beans

1 cup finely chopped walnuts

2/3 cup sugar

1 tablespoon butter

Chocolate fudge frosting (page 48)

Chocolate-covered espresso beans, to serve (optional)

1. Preheat the oven to 350°F. Prepare two 8 x 8-inch baking dishes.

2. Combine the cake mix, oil, eggs, 1 cup coffee, melted chocolate, and 1 tablespoon ground coffee in a large bowl and blend with an electric mixer on medium speed for about 2 minutes.

3. Fold in the walnuts and divide the batter evenly between the two prepared dishes. Bake in the center of the oven for 35 to 40 minutes, until a toothpick inserted into the center comes out clean.

4. While the pans are baking, put the 2/3 cup coffee, sugar, and butter into a small saucepan, bring to a boil over medium heat, then reduce to a simmer and continue to cook for about 5 minutes.

5. As soon as the bars come out of the oven, pour the coffee syrup over them. Cool completely before turning out of the pans. With a very sharp knife, cut each cake into 16 equal squares.

6. Make the fudge frosting, blending in the remaining 1 tablespoon ground coffee and use to frost the tops and sides of each square. Top each frosted square with a chocolate-covered espresso bean and place on a small paper doily.

Handy Hint: When buying the coffee beans, grind them on the espresso setting or, better yet, the Turkish coffee setting.

Notes

Index